The Diaconate Of Women In The Anglican Church

THE DIACONATE OF WOMEN

IN,

THE ANGLICAN CHURCH.

THE DIACONATE OF WOMEN

IN

THE ANGLICAN CHURCH.

*FIVE CHAPTERS ON THE PRESENT ATTITUDE
OF THE QUESTION.*

BY THE
VERY REV. J. S. HOWSON, D.D.
LATE DEAN OF CHESTER.

WITH

A SHORT BIOGRAPHICAL SKETCH BY HIS SON.

LONDON:
JAMES NISBET & CO., 21 BERNERS STREET.
MDCCCLXXXVI.

ALD
BV
4424
.C5
H6
1886

PREFACE.

THE chapters which follow are really detached addresses, delivered on various occasions: but each has a distinct character of its own, and deals with a separate aspect of the subject to which this volume relates.

It is a subject upon which I think I have acquired by persistency some right to express my opinions. In the year 1860 I had obtained strong convictions regarding it, after taking great pains to procure information. And this state of mind was permitted to make itself known in the *Quarterly Review* of September in that year. That article led to remarkable results, and especially to the founding of the first Deaconess Institution of the Church of England. And here I must speak with respectful and affectionate remembrance of Elizabeth Ferad, the first Deaconess of our Church. The real meaning of the question was quickly seen by that great Prelate, Bishop Tait, who sanctioned regulations and services, and gave unreserved and official appointment along with the strength of his sympathy.

Now here it is to be observed that the ministry in question is contemplated as a Church ministry. Not one word is said in disparagement or in praise of sisters, of nurses, of district visitors, of Bible-women, of Zenana workers, &c. &c.

If a few words are written in succession on the aspects of the subject touched in these separate addresses, and on the occasions when they were delivered, the case will become very clear.

The first chapter contains an address delivered on the general Biblical aspect of the Ministry of Women, delivered at Farnham Castle at a meeting of Deaconesses arranged with great kindness and most happy results. The new position of dignity, service, and responsibility to which women has been brought by the Gospel must lie at the base of this whole question. We do not yet see the end of this mighty change, but one thing appears to me very certain, that it is a great mistake to subordinate the Biblical aspect of this subject to the ecclesiastical.

In the second chapter, which contains a paper read at the Reading Church Congress, we come upon ecclesiastical ground. The subject of female ministration in the Church has been debated at several such Congresses since a very memorable discussion at Oxford, in the year 1862: and it cannot be doubted that public opinion regarding it has in this way been gradually enriched and matured.

With the third chapter we enter upon debates on this question in Convocation at York. I brought this matter forward there under a strong feeling of the deep necessity of a ministry of this kind, and with a hope of a good discussion and the adopting of some practical step. In these hopes I was not disappointed. The debate was very animated, and a committee was appointed with full powers to draw up a complete report on the service of women in the Church of England under various points of view.

My own share in the preparation of this report had special reference to the history of the Diaconate of Women in primitive times. It unfortunately happened that my condition of health prevented me from making this part of the document as complete as I could have wished. This led to the separate printing of the pamphlet which constitutes the fourth chapter. I hope the reading of it will show clearly that we have still much to learn from these early sources. But on two points I venture to express a very strong opinion—1st, that a Diaconate of Women as an apostolical institution is inherent in the Church; 2dly, that traces of its existence through long periods are quite sufficient to justify the resumption of it, whenever it should be found expedient to do so.

The last chapter contains an account of the further steps that were taken in Convocation at York as an introduction to the speech which I made on presenting the report. Once more the debate was very serious and complete; and a practical point was reached from which I hope that large and beneficial results will follow.

The book which was published in 1860 has been long out of print, and I have been asked to republish it, with or without modifications. Such a task is quite impossible at the present time; and I am inclined to think that this is a case to which the old Greek poet's proverb is applicable, "that the half is greater than the whole." At all events I am sanguine enough to hope that these few pages, sent forth with prayer, may lead to wide thought, and to actual progress in a cause of the utmost moment to our English Church.

CONTENTS.

	PAGE
PREFACE	v
SHORT BIOGRAPHICAL SKETCH	xiii
BIBLICAL ASPECTS OF THE MINISTRY OF WOMEN	1
DEACONESSES	24
THE CHURCH MINISTRY OF WOMEN	42
THE PRIMITIVE DIACONATE OF WOMEN	59
SPEECH	80

A SHORT BIOGRAPHICAL SKETCH.

THERE is a sentence which appears on page 6 of this little book which will suggest to its readers solemn thought. My father there says of that work which he had so much at heart, that doubtless the diaconate of women will have found a far more lasting place than at present in the work of the Christian Church when "some of us are in our graves." Since that was written he and my mother have entered that rest "which remaineth for the people of God." The voice which pleaded for "woman's work in the Church" is now silent; but what he has written in this book will echo that appeal in no uncertain, unhesitating tone.

My father, John Saul Howson, was born at Giggleswick, in Yorkshire, in May 1816.[*] His

[*] He was always proud of the fact of his being a Yorkshireman, and one of the last things I remember his speaking of was the coincidence at the consecration of the present Bishop of Chester,

father was at the head of the grammar-school in that village, which has increased its influence in later years. His mother was a Miss Saul, after whose family he was named,—a name singularly prophetic of the hero of so many of his books in after days. I may quote from a short autobiography which he prepared for the Giggleswick school newspaper a very little while before he died, to give an idea of his boyhood:—

"I was never fond of games, . . . but I remember playing marbles by the hour with a boy named Whitaker, who was my dear and intimate friend. . . . I fancy we both were very full of boyish poetry. . . . He was nearer heaven than I was, in more senses than one. . . . I am sorry to say I was very passionate. . . . It was a great disadvantage to me that I was at the head of the school at a very early age. . . . I was idle and desultory, and my father thought that the severe conflict to which I should be exposed by being sent to Cambridge at the early age of seventeen would have a bracing effect on me. So far he was right. . . .

that at the same service in York Minster, the Dean, the Bishop, and the preacher (Dr. Kay) were all Yorkshiremen, born within a very few miles of one another.

Before I leave my boyhood I ought to add that my father's botanical tastes led me to an early study of plants, which has been of the utmost service to me ever since." *

Again I quote some words from the autobiography:—

"My mother died in the autumn of 1834, when I was spending my first long vacation at home. I had the comfort of being with her constantly during her last painful illness. . . . I remember her saying to me that I had never caused her a moment's anxiety. I wondered then, as I wonder now, at a mother's power of forgetting."

After school-days he went to Trinity, Cambridge, on obtaining a scholarship. He was younger than his contemporaries by some two years, and his career at college was therefore all the more remarkable. Suffice it to say that his degree was a double first, that he obtained the Member's prize in 1837 and 1838, and the Norrisian prize, 1840. He took his M.A. degree in 1841, and D.D. *honoris causâ* in 1861. During the five years which passed before he was ordained he was tutor to the

---

* His romantic love of nature was with him to the last. Had he lived, he wished his first sermon to be on the subject of Spring.

Marquis of Lorne, now Duke of Argyll, to the Marquis of Sligo, and to the Marquis of Stafford, now Duke of Sutherland. The work of his early years was in conjunction with the late Rev. W. J. Conybeare, both as joint-author of the "Life and Epistles of St. Paul," and in the management and teaching of the then new Collegiate Institution at Liverpool.

That a book which is now looked upon as of a classical type should have been the work of two young clergymen is in itself a sign of the ability of each. It was published in the year 1852. Mr. Conybeare supplied the translations of some of the Epistles, my father undertook the historical and geographical portions, and in this particular it was that the most solid addition was made to the existing means of realising and understanding the Apostolical age. I may quote from an article in the *Times* the criticism of one authority:—" In the elucidation of the missionary journeys of St. Paul, first of their kind in the world's history, there is no resource of topographical knowledge, from Chandler and Beaufort, from Tournefort and Hamilton, from numismatic collections or Admiralty charts, that Mr. Howson has not successfully ransacked. Classical no less than Biblical scholars may turn with advantage to his pages for the intricate divisions, never so clearly set forth, of the provinces of Asia Minor; the graphic descriptions, never before so fully compiled, of the deep glens of Cilicia and the wild upland hollows of Pisidia and Lycaonia."

It was a delight to my father to remember the oft-repeated question, "Of course you have been over the ground thus described?" and to answer, "No, only a small part; I hope before I die I shall have seen the whole." That hope was, I believe, thoroughly fulfilled when he took his journey to the East some three years ago.

The work of clearing the affairs of the Institution at Liverpool from debt, and of giving it new impetus, was begun during the years of his principalship, 1849 to 1865, and he had on one occasion, which I remember well, the joy of knowing that over 900 pupils were under his supervision in the three divisions of Liverpool College. Sixteen, nearly seventeen, years of exhausting, never-ceasing work in Liverpool obliged him to resign the appointment in 1866.

It will be seen from the preface of this little book that it was first in 1861 that the subject of how to promote the systematic ministry of women engaged his attention. He began then, what during twenty-five years of his life he rarely let slip, to use every opportunity of advocating a ministry of women trained for the work it had to do, acting in harmony with parochial arrangements, and under the sanction of the bishops, but yet flexible and free, elastic, yet quietly controlled, and suited to the needs of various institutions. The establishment of the Deaconess Institution in Liverpool has led to the organising of many others in other parts of England.

In 1866 the present Bishop of Winchester, then Bishop of Ely, whose examining chaplain he was to the end of his life, appointed my father to the Vicarage of Wisbech, an important but to him almost new kind of work. One year there saw, at any rate, one great thing done in the building of a new church in the large parish of St. Peter, and I know that he looked back upon that time of parochial work as a most valuable addition to his experience, and to his power of sympathy in all Christian undertakings.

When Dr. Anson, who had been Dean of Chester for many years, died, the late Lord Derby appointed my father to succeed him. In those days a deanery was looked upon as an opportunity for quietness and rest, for contemplation and for meditation; but in that, as in every other office work, it is true that it is not the office that makes the man, but the man who makes the office; and especially true was it of him who, till a few weeks ago, was Dean of Chester. Fulsomeness in praise of his work coming from the pen of his son would seem an insult to his memory; yet it must be said that few men have succeeded in four years in getting together no less than £40,000 for the restoration of a cathedral that used to be considered insignificant and squalid, and scarcely worth the expenditure, but which now is acknowledged by all who visit it as one of the grandest instances of restored beauty.

Two objects were before my father in founding the cathedral when he came to Chester. The first was the erecting of something unknown; the second was the restoring of something unseen. "He held," and again I use words other than my own, "that it was a great mistake to look upon English cathedrals as merely churches for the celebration of a solemn and stately worship. They were indeed this, but also much more than this. A noble cathedral's foundations were, in his view, intended to be, and well adapted to become, schools of sacred music, centres of healthy religious influence, homes of theological learning, places of useful education, helps alike to church business and missionary activity."

In accordance with these views, one of the first things he did was to establish a choral Sunday-evening service in the nave. This service has proved an immense blessing to Chester; and though at first it seemed likely to rob some of the parish churches of their evening congregation, the event has proved that, instead of this being the result, those who had been in the habit of attending no service were drawn to the cathedral, while the parish churches have recovered their congregations in almost every case.

The Musical Festival, annual choral festivals for the diocese, services for the various diocesan institutions, all found a home in the cathedral, so that there was nothing that could promote the good, spiritual, moral, or educational, which did not find a response in this the centre of the church-life in the diocese.

The restoration of the fabric, however, is that which will stand for a continual memorial of my father's work in Chester; £100,000 spent in ten years has naturally produced a complete alteration in the building. He found the cathedral in a most dilapidated state, in many cases in a most dangerous condition, and in conjunction with Sir Gilbert Scott he has left it a glory of the diocese. The words commemorative of Sir Christopher Wren are true indeed of him, "*Si monumentum quæris, circumspice.*"

A long-waited-for completion he was permitted to see, and it was his last public act to join in the dedication service. At the north-west corner of the nave stood the old Bishop's Palace, built in and upon some most beautiful Norman masonry. This was opened out and a noble baptistery conceived. In it was placed an Italian font of great beauty, the gift of a noble layman in the diocese,* and the floor of tesselated mosaic representing the Draught of Fishes (a favourite idea with my father) he designed. This was dedicated during his illness, and his last words in the cathedral he so dearly loved were spoken then. Ill as he was, his voice was as clear as ever, and strongly did he plead for greater reverence and importance to be attached to the "blessed sacrament" of baptism.

* Lord Egerton of Tatton.

I have omitted to mention the other schemes that he set on foot or resuscitated during his residence in Chester. The increased usefulness of Naidan's Theological College was his work; the enlarged sphere of work for the King's School at Chester, to which he gave the motto "*Rex dedit benedicat Deus;*" the establishment of the Queen's School for girls on the same lines as one he originated in Liverpool; the reviving of the interest in archæology and antiquarian research, are amongst some of the things by which he will be remembered.

I cannot help thinking that he felt that his work of activity in the world was drawing to its close a year or two ago; for often he used to say, "I want to give the rest of my life to devotional writing and practical spiritual good. I do not wish to enter any more into the world of controversy; I must leave that to others." The last two books, which appeared just at the time of his death, are instances of this wish. Still he died "in harness." On the Sunday week before he entered into his rest he had finished the work of handing over all the care of the cathedral into other hands; and when he had done this, it seemed that his active life was done. "Rest and peace for me," were some of his last words; and indeed that was a true experience.

It was a touching incident in his last hours that a book* he had much looked forward to publishing should have arrived the night before he died, and the first copy of which he had intended for my mother. She, who had with lovely devotion, in spite of her severe accident, travelled hither, was brought to his bedside at his whispered request, and he with great difficulty placed it in her hands. The other,† which was to appear at the same time, came from the publisher the night before my mother was called home.

In the second of these two volumes, the last chapter is devoted to the subject of the death of a Christian in its aspect of "Sleep in Jesus," and it closes with words most indicative of his own life: "David, after he had served his own generation, by the will of God, fell on sleep." I cannot refrain from giving a sketch of a sermon he himself gave me just before my ordination on that text, to show what it seems must have been constantly before him as his ideal of Christian service:—

* Our Collects, Epistles, and Gospels.
† Thoughts for Saints' Days.

Introduction.—Here we have St. Paul's view of the life and death of David. The view by any great man of another is sure to be interesting.

(1.) Life *a service.* "Whose I am and whom I serve." "I *serve* the Lord Christ."

(2.) *Sphere of service.* Our own generation God's appointed place.

(3.) *Consecrating principle of service.* The will of God.

(4.) *Its end and reward.* Falling asleep. Compare the expression used of the death of Stephen.

Conclusion—Exhortation that our life should be in accordance with this.

He entered into his well-earned rest on the afternoon of the 15th of December 1885. He literally fell on sleep; for during the last twenty-four hours he was gently sleeping away, with no pain, none of the restless activity disturbing his peace which had characterised the earlier part of his illness. His body was taken from Bournemouth to Chester, and now lies with that of my mother, who followed him but fifteen days after, in the south-east corner of the cloister green. No one who was present at the solemn service could help feeling how beautiful and hallowed a resting-place was reserved for his body who had toiled so long and lovingly in and for the cathedral.

How beautifully appropriate are these words of Bernard de Morlaix to him—

> "Post nigra, post mala, post fera scandala quæ caro præstat,
> Absque nigredine lux, sine turbine pax tibi restat,
> Sunt modo prælia, post modo præmia. Qualia? Plena,
> Plena refectio, nullaque passio, nullaque pœna."

Perhaps a son may be allowed to mark some characteristics of his father's life as an example to all time, though he shrinks from criticising the personal goodness of his character. Two grand features in my father's life seem to be characteristic of him. The first was this: A strong idea of self-control, and of that sobriety of which he speaks on page 20 of this little book. The second was his habit of doing things thoroughly and without waste of time. As an instance of this fact, I may just quote a thing he used often to say: "Always try to do things with both hands." And to indicate the latter habit, "I have often written a sermon amongst the oil-cans and tow in the porter's cabin by a roadside station." In these days thoroughness and completeness are the very things which many well-disposed Christians sadly lack.

Of his personal character let others well known to him and to the world speak. "I shall always think of your father as one of the *very whitest souls* I have met in the course of my pilgrimage." . . . "You must console yourselves with the thought that few men in this generation will part with a father whose life was of equal value, whose character was so noble and Christian, and who leaves behind him such permanent memorials of his life." . . . "There was a moderation in spite of his zeal, a charity towards others, notwithstanding the strength of his convictions as he opposed them, and a peculiar freshness which one does not often find in men of his age. We shall sorely miss him in council; the Church will miss him; but above all, how will not you all miss him!" "Life is a much poorer and sadder business to me from the death of one who has been to me like a kindly sunshine." "A beautiful character; a life at once studious, sociable, and practical—a life given to useful labour in writing and educating, and a Churchmanship earnest without narrowness, and liberal without vagueness."

G. J. H.

OVERTON RECTORY, *February* 1886.

Postscript.—The following is as nearly as possible a complete list of his writings:—" Life and Epistles of St. Paul." " Scenes from the Life of St. Paul." " Companions of St. Paul." " Character of St. Paul." " Metaphors of St. Paul." " Meditations on the Miracles of Christ," two volumes. " Deaconesses." " On Collects, Epistles, and Gospels." " Thoughts for Saints' Days." " Before the Table." " Sacramental Confession." " Sermons to Schoolboys." " Short Sermons for Family Reading." " Alms and Oblations." " Good and Bad Habits." " Hagar and Arabia." " Moses Succeeded by Joshua." " Voyage in the Mediterranean." " Our own Things and the Things of Others." " The Way to do Harm and the Way to do Good." " Proportion in Religious Belief and Religious Practices." " Chester as it was.". " The River Dee and its History." " Notes Devotional and Historical" (for the Chester Festival.)

He contributed to Smith's " Dictionary of the Bible," " The Speaker's Commentary," " Essays on Cathedrals," and to the leading Reviews.

BIBLICAL ASPECTS OF THE MINISTRY OF WOMEN.

AN ADDRESS DELIVERED AT A MEETING OF DEACONESSES IN FARNHAM CASTLE, ON THE 26TH DAY OF JULY 1883.

HAVING before me in prospect the duty which I am now about to try to discharge, and feeling seriously all the responsibility of the occasion, I determined to limit myself to the ground of the New Testament. When we are thinking of religious subjects, we find no freshness like the freshness of the Holy Scriptures. Whatever other streams of spiritual help there may be, for instruction, for edification, and for comfort—and they are many, and very precious—"behold," when we have the Bible close at our side, "we stand by the well of water."[1]

And there is another reason for this limitation. We stand thus on the ground of safety. We cannot

[1] Gen. xxiv. 13.

conceal from ourselves that there are many difficulties connected with this subject of the Ministry of Women in the Church. This is not the moment for the discussion of such difficulties; and, after all, they are, for the most part, either personal, on the one hand, or ecclesiastical on the other. They are not Biblical difficulties. In this respect, as in others, we are conscious of the value of the truth that is set before us in that hundred and nineteenth Psalm, which is a guide to our devotions on this day: "Thy Word is a lantern unto my feet, and a light unto my paths." [1]

Thus I believe I cannot make a mistake if I select three illustrations of the Religious Ministry of Women from the Gospels, three from the Acts of the Apostles, and three from the Epistles. In this way we shall be travelling in the footsteps of our Lord and His immediate followers. The symmetry too may be, for some of us, a help to the memory: while it will certainly remind us of the wide diffusion of this topic through the Scriptures of the New Testament.

[1] Ps. cxix. 105.

I.—(1.) On the very threshold of the Gospel history, and in the midst of those sacred Canticles which we use in our Public Worship, we meet with an illustrative example which is full of meaning. At the time of our Saviour's first presentation in the Temple, at the moment of the uttering of the *Nunc Dimittis*, we find a man and a woman alike in readiness.[1] Each sex is represented on equal terms. Even this bare fact is very significant. The Gospel history tells us without delay of the high dignity to which woman has been raised, while at the same time we are conscious of the utmost tenderness of feeling in this picture of Anna's long-continued sorrow.

She had waited many years. Her example is an example of patience. And yet she exhibits too, for our benefit, another side of character in close union with this. After the mention of her "giving of thanks in like manner with Simeon," it is said immediately that she "spake of the Lord to all them that looked for redemption in Jerusalem." Doubtless she knew them well. During those long years of waiting she must have become acquainted

[1] St. Luke ii. 36-38.

with many whose desires and hopes were like her own. And they must often have "spoken together, while the Lord hearkened and heard."[1] Now she loses not a moment in proclaiming the good news, and in gladdening those hearts. It might be truly said that Anna was the first Christian Evangelist, the first Christian missionary. It is this combination of alacrity with patience which constitutes her so admirable an example of the Deaconess-spirit.

This instance receives some additional force, when we remember that Anna was "of the tribe of Assher,"—a tribe of no fame and distinction, but, on the contrary, a somewhat ignoble and subordinate tribe. It is hardly mentioned at all in Hebrew history. Hardly any person is named as belonging to it, except in mere lists of genealogy. But the incident which we have before us here raises this tribe to an honour almost equal to that of any of the rest. And we ought to carry this thought with us into the reading of the Book of Revelation, where, amid the hundred and forty-four thousand of "the servants of our God," no difference among the tribes

---

[1] Malachi iii. 16.

is made, but "of the tribe of Assher were sealed twelve thousand."[1]

(2.) Activity and patience are again visibly side by side, when the examples of Martha and Mary are before us. Not, however, in this instance, combined in the same person: and one lesson of that eleventh chapter of St. John's Gospel is this, that they ought to be so combined. But such instruction has very often been drawn from this passage, and I will turn to other aspects of this scene at Bethany.

We cannot fail to observe, in the first place, how great a position the scene occupies in the section of the Evangelic history. We feel that it is characteristic of the Fourth Gospel; and herein it has done much to raise to its proper level our estimate of the high place of woman in the Christian Church.

But another point to be well marked is the discipline of sorrow in the experience of this family of Bethany. Anna, of whom we have already been thinking, had this discipline in one way. Martha and Mary had it in another. If there is to be a system of Deaconesses pervading the Church of England—as I expect there will be, when some of

[1] Rev. vii. 4-8.

us are in our graves—some of the best strength of this system will be supplied by those who have suffered much, and who through sanctified suffering have learnt to speak words of wisdom and moderation, and to exercise a sober controlling influence on others who are too vehement and eager.

And once more, Bethany admonishes us of the sacredness of domestic life. In the suggestions regarding the ministry of women, which the New Testament provides, there is nothing monastic. Some conclusions in this direction might possibly, with ingenuity, be drawn from what is said in the Acts of the Apostles concerning Philip's daughters,[1] and from a remark concerning the official "widows" in one of the Pastoral Epistles.[2] But I do not think that inferences of this kind amount to much; whereas the inculcation in the New Testament, directly and indirectly, of the sacredness of domestic life, amounts to very much indeed; and the Divine blessing could not confidently be expected, if a system of Deaconesses in the Church were organised in forgetfulness of this truth.

(3.) We turn now to another of the Four Gospels,

[1] Acts xxi. 9.   [2] 1 Tim. v. 12.

and to a very different illustration of the service of women in the cause of Christ. This is the description given, in more places than one, of the Galilean women; and we observe that it is given by that Evangelist whose Gospel is marked by such sympathetic reference to women, especially widows.[1]

Why such high honour should have been assigned to Galilee in the first planting of the Gospel upon this earth, we may not be able fully to explain—though some true parts of the explanation might perhaps easily be furnished. Here I refer simply to the fact, which is undoubted. Alike at the beginning and at the end of the sacred history of Christ, Galilee was chosen as the consecrated place of holy teaching and wondrous miracles, and as the starting-point for all the future history of the Church.[2] The loving associations of the first days seem to have been renewed after the Resurrection.[3] But the point before our notice now is that this general glory of Galilee is expressly connected with women. Both early and late we see Galilean women "ministering" to Jesus.

---

[1] St. Luke ii. 37; iv. 25; vii. 13; xviii. 3-5.
[2] Acts x. 37.
[3] St. Matt. xxvi. 32; xxviii. 16; St. John xxi. 1.

And this word "ministering" leads to another remark which deserves consideration. It is, in the original, the very word from whence is derived the designation of the office which gives occasion to our meeting to-day. It expresses all that helping, loving service, which has been so great a blessing to the world, age after age. On several occasions the word is used in this connection.[1] For instance, St. Mark says of the women at the Cross—using the same word,—that "when Jesus was in Galilee they had followed Him and ministered to Him."[2] Thus we seem to have here the consecration of an ecclesiastical term very full of meaning.

But the remembrance of these Galilean women must carry us to a point beyond mere local and verbal questions. Their lavish self-sacrifice—their endurance of fatigue—their forgetfulness of danger—all this is characteristic of the devotion of women. We see this alike during the early days in Galilee, and at the Saviour's Tomb at Jerusalem. They make no calculation of consequences. They disregard all difficulties. Such zeal is very beautiful, very inspir-

---

[1] St. Matt. viii. 15; St. John xii. 2.
[2] St. Mark xv. 41.

ing. It often secures success, when mere prudence would fail: and it kindles the zeal of others, so that they accomplish what they thought impossible.

II.—(1.) In the early part of the Apostolic history we are taken, while following this line of thought, to another part of the Holy Land. English travellers to that land commonly disembark at Joppa and proceed to Lydda. St. Peter's route between these two places was in the opposite direction.[1] What is described as taking place at Joppa on his arrival from Lydda deserves our most careful attention. The mere fact that the story of Dorcas is recorded is important: and we should mark the place which it occupies, between the account of the Conversion of St. Paul on the one hand, and the account of the Conversion of Cornelius on the other. It is as if the sacred narrative paused in its stately march, for the sake of this quiet lesson of beneficence; even as the Lord Jesus, when He was on one of His public errands of mercy, paused for the healing and blessing of a solitary sufferer by the way.[2]

The name of Dorcas itself seems to bring the

[1] Acts ix. 32–43. [2] St. Luke viii. 46.

scene very closely in contact with our commonest experience. And such conscious contact with the Bible history is a great advantage. It elevates our simple deeds of benevolence, when we see that such deeds were even honoured by a miracle.

But at this point a thought occurs to me, to which I cannot help giving expression. Who were those "widows" that stood by weeping when Peter entered the chamber of the dead? When Dorcas was restored to life, it is said that "he called the saints and widows."[1] Were not these widows saints? Were they not Christians? It seems as if some distinction were drawn between them and the other saints or Christians. What if we have here the germ of that ministry of official "widows," which, as we know from the Pastoral Epistles, was afterwards more fully developed and organised?[2] And these suggestions lead our thoughts to a further point. Who were those "widows" that were "neglected in the daily ministration," so that murmuring on their account led to the appointment of St. Stephen and his six companions?[3] I confess I would rather believe that they were women appointed to the task of distri-

[1] Acts ix. 41.   [2] 1 Tim. v. 5–10.   [3] Acts vi. 1.

buting alms than that they were complaining recipients of alms. If these things were so, the earliest ministry in the Church would be a Ministry of Women. I will not dogmatise regarding that which can be only conjecture. But this at least is remarkable (and it is not foreign to our subject), that it is Philanthropy in the midst of which the first notices of the Christian Ministry occur. And this is the case not only with regard to the Deacons, but the Presbyters also; for the first mention of them is simply this:—" The disciples at Antioch determined to send relief to their brethren in Judea, which also they did, and sent it to the Elders by the hands of Barnabus and Saul."[1] Philanthropy is the very mission of the Deaconess: and it is an encouragement to her to see it thus treated in Scripture with the highest honour.

(2.) We now turn to places which are far from Palestine, and are in different parts of the missionary journeys of St. Paul. Of the church at Philippi it has often been remarked that the presence of women in connection with it is made very prominent. This topic will be mentioned again, when occasion arises

[1] Acts xi. 29, 30.

for the quoting of that Epistle to the Philippians which was written very long after St. Paul's earliest visit to Macedonia. But that earliest visit is full of suggestion for our present thoughts.

And first let us call to mind that this is the earliest introduction of Christianity into Europe. The arrival at Philippi is a step of the most momentous kind in the progress of the Gospel. Is it not a notable fact that the first encouragement came from a small company of women?[1] It seems as if everywhere in the inspired record women were set before us—very modestly indeed, yet very decisively —in a high position of opportunity and usefulness for the evangelisation of the world.

Let us observe very carefully the extreme simplicity and quietness of this meeting of Lydia and her companions by the river-side. Nothing could be more unobtrusive. Yet from this small commencement spread that vast spiritual power which subdued our continent, which caused a revolution in human thought, which commanded kings, which tamed barbarians, which raised the oppressed, and

[1] Acts xvi. 13.

which has descended in blessing even to our times. Surely this is an admonition to us—an admonition we sorely need—not to despise small beginnings.

Above all we must remember that it was in prayer that this evangelisation of Europe began; and it is in prayer that this evangelisation must continue. It is prayer which is the best feature of this our present meeting.

(3.) There seems no imperative reason for imagining that Dorcas and Lydia were women of great powers or striking character. They may, for anything we know, have been persons of very average ability. We can, however, as it seems to me, hardly say this of Priscilla. The manner in which she is mentioned appears to give the impression that she was a woman of more than ordinary gifts, with a vigorous power of exerting influence over others. We find her conspicuous in three separate places, widely distant from one another—Corinth, Ephesus, and Rome.[1] We find her generous and fearless in hospitality. "The Church in their house" is a phrase which belongs pre-eminently to Aquila and

---

[1] Acts xviii. 2, 3, 19; Rom. xvi. 3, 4; 1 Cor. xvi. 19; 2 Tim. iv. 19.

Priscilla. "All the Churches of the Gentiles" are spoken of as their debtors. In some way, perhaps on more occasions than one, they had exposed themselves to signal danger on behalf of St. Paul. Above all we find Priscilla as the instructor of a highly-gifted young man, so that under her he became better fitted to teach the Gospel to others.[1]

Now on this two remarks must be made. This devoted woman probably did in many other instances what she did in the instances recorded. We cannot too carefully remember that in the New Testament we have only fragments of biography, and that in such a case as this we have merely samples of a wide range of successful work. Hence the duty of studying very carefully what is so full of suggestion.

But further, we must call to mind that domestic life among the Greeks was very secluded. Hence the case of Priscilla introduces us to the Missionary aspect of feminine service. She is seen at work, as it were, in the zenanas of the ancient world. What is wanted now was wanted then. She was the forerunner of many women of great power and deep

[1] Acts xviii. 26.

devotion, who have lived since; and great is the blessing to the Church and to the world, when such "a mother in Israel"[1] is granted to live among us.

III. (1.) The Bishop of Durham has remarked, in his recent Charge, that, according to the word of Scripture, Phœbe has as full a right to be termed a "deacon" as have Stephen and Philip. But, in fact, the case might with truth have been stated much more strongly; for neither Stephen nor Philip is ever designated as a "deacon," whereas Priscilla is distinctly so designated. In fact, she is the only person in the New Testament who appears by name under this designation.[2] She is spoken of in exactly the language which we find to be customary in the ages that immediately succeeded the Apostolic time. There we find the "man-deacon" and the "woman-deacon" as co-ordinate members of the same general ministry. The same word served for both; and wherever we find correspondence between the language of early Church history and the language of the New Testament, our reverent attention is urgently claimed.

[1] Judges v. 7. [2] Rom. xvi. 1, 2.

In St. Paul's manner of mentioning Phœbe there is a warm personal feeling which indicates the recollection of some service rendered to himself—"She hath been a succourer of many, and of myself also." Now Phœbe was "a Deaconess of the Church of Cenchreæ;" and we find that Paul, at a previous time, had bound himself, according to an old Jewish custom, by a Nazarite vow at this seaport.[1] It is not unnatural to suppose that this vow had some reference to the recovery of health. Perhaps Phœbe had helped him with her care during a time of sickness. This would have been true Deaconess-work. If this conjecture is correct, then there is a gratitude here in St. Paul's language similar to the gratitude which finds expression elsewhere in a reference to "the beloved Physician."[2] It was on this same missionary journey, that, as we are reminded by the Revised Version of the New Testament, St. Paul was detained by sickness in Galatia;[3] and it was immediately after this time that he met St. Luke at Troas.[4] Loving and useful service which has been rendered in a time of suffering is rewarded by a

[1] Acts xviii. 18.   [2] Col. iv. 14.
[3] Gal. iv. 13.   [4] Acts xvi. 10.

permanent blessing, and abounds afterwards by many thanksgivings unto God.

If we thus mark carefully the place from which Phœbe came, we should mark with equal care the place to which she was sent. A voyage from the neighbourhood of Corinth to Rome was at that time attended with far greater difficulty and fatigue than at present. Such difficulty and fatigue give point to one part of the example. This solitary errand, thus bravely undertaken, illustrates the duties which a Deaconess in the Church may be called upon to discharge. St. Paul says to the Roman Christians concerning Phœbe, that they are to "assist her in whatsoever business she had need of them;" and certainly it is our duty on behalf of all who thus courageously exercise their feminine ministry, that we make their tasks as easy as we can, and that we surround them with respectful sympathy.

(2.) That Epistle to the Philippians, to which I referred before, begins in a remarkable manner. In the opening salutation the Apostle, contrary to his usual custom, addresses particularly the "bishops and deacons."[1] Did these "deacons" include

[1] Phil. i. 1.

women? Were the two co-ordinate sections of the Helping Ministry established at Philippi? I think it probable that the answer to these two questions ought to be affirmative. I will not, however, pursue the inquiry, but will proceed at once to a request which is preferred by St. Paul to two women who are named in the Epistle, and who, most probably, were members of the Diaconate.

"I beseech Euodia and beseech Syntyche, that they be of the same mind in the Lord."[1] There had been some failure in the maintenance of harmony between these two women; and there is a most striking reiteration and symmetry in the form of the appeal. The word "beseech" is twice repeated. Probably we should not be far wrong, if we were to infer from this that there was fault on both sides. This is commonly the case, when a serious misunderstanding occurs. Certainly when any such occurrence takes place, self-examination is a duty on each side—for certainly want of harmony sadly hinders the efficiency, and tarnishes the dignity, of Christian work. The rules for conducting such self-examination are very simple. We should do unto

[1] Phil. iv. 2.

others "as we would that they should do unto us,"[1] and each should "esteem other better than herself."[2]

And the words which follow deserve our careful notice. The "true yokefellow" may have been Epaphroditus or St. Luke. We need not attempt to settle that question. The appeal to him is this— "help those women, because they laboured with me in the Gospel." So the turn of the sentence is correctly given in the Revised Version. The fact that there was want of harmony was no reason why their good and useful co-operation in the work of the Gospel should not be recognised. On the contrary it was the strongest reason why all that tended to spoil that work should be removed. We need not, indeed, limit the word "help" here to efforts for reconciliation, though primarily, no doubt, it has that reference. And no efforts are more worthy of being patiently made. "Blessed are the peacemakers; for they shall be called the children of God."[3]

(3.) Allusion has been twice made to the Revised Version. And now, when we come to our last

[1] Matt. vii. 12.   [2] Phil. ii. 3.   [3] St. Matt. v. 9.

Biblical illustration, we find that this new revision has rescued a very important passage from serious error. I will not argue concerning the meaning of the sentence we must select from the passage in the First Epistle to Timothy,[1] where St. Paul describes the qualifications of those who are worthy to be admitted into the ministries of the Church. Having strong convictions on the subject, after having thought about it for many years, I will merely note three features of character, which are set forth there as recommendations for the Female Diaconate.

First, there is to be "gravity" of outward demeanour. This does not mean gloom: but it does mean seriousness and simplicity. As to anything like levity, this—with so much sorrow, so much sin all around us—must surely be impossible.

And the next qualification is "sobriety" of mind. Nothing can be more essential in such a calling, than the maintaining of a just balance, the possession of "a right judgment in all things," the observing of due proportion, firm resistance to mere impulse, the avoiding of extremes, and, above all, the avoiding of inconsistency.

[1] 1 Tim. i

MINISTRY OF WOMEN.

Finally, "trustworthiness" in all things. So I understand the word "faithful" in this passage. It must be confessed, with much sadness of heart, that lack of strict truthfulness may be combined with most earnest devotion. When we have a point to gain, in a matter of religion, we may sometimes be tempted to be less scrupulous than we ought to be in the manner of obtaining our end. Thus God is dishonoured, our conscience is weakened and lowered, and where the utmost confidence ought to subsist, distrust is created. "Let your yea be yea, and your nay, nay," says the Great Master.[1]

Thus from various scenes named in Scripture—from Jerusalem, from Bethany, from Galilee, from Joppa—we have gathered instances of the loving, faithful devotion of women to Christ; from various places visited by Christ's Apostle—from Corinth, from Ephesus, from Philippi, from Rome—we have collected instances of the early establishment of a Female Diaconate in the Church. I venture to add Rome; for I cannot but believe that some of those who are named in the last chapter of the Epistle to the Romans, must have belonged to the Diaconate.

[1] St. Matt. v. 37; St. James v. 12.

This thought was in my mind, when, a few years ago, I saw the names "Tryphæna and Tryphosa,"[1] on monuments belonging to "Cæsar's household."[2] However this may be, we cannot doubt that we have had before us a great principle of the New Testament, unobtrusive, indeed, but pervading, and therefore demanding the most serious study.

I ventured to say above that I think we are in a crisis of the question. I do not see how any one, who looks carefully around, can fail to see indications of this. Some parts of this great subject may, before long, attract attention in very serious forms. All this ought to make us feel our responsibility, to make us ready to inquire and willing to learn, to dispose us to patience, to quicken our prayers.

And, for one last word, I will say that no woman, however lowly her estimate of herself, ought to doubt that she may do much good at such a time. Great capabilities indeed—such as may have been possessed by Priscilla and Phœbe—are gifts of God. But great opportunities may be granted to such as Anna and Lydia. His Providence must guide us.

[1] Rom. xvi. 12.   [2] Phil. iv. 22.

His Holy Spirit must teach us. "In quietness and in confidence must be our strength."[1] May He give to us, in this troubled time, the blessing of "a quiet mind!" May His strength "be made perfect in our weakness!"[2]

[1] Isaiah xxx. 15.   [2] 2 Cor. xii. 9.

DEACONESSES.

A PAPER READ AT THE CHURCH CONGRESS HELD IN READING, OCTOBER 1883.

I find it quite impossible to read this paper without calling seriously and vividly to mind the discussion of the same subject at the Church Congress of 1862, in this Diocese. That was for two reasons a remarkable occasion. In the first place this very institution of the Church Congress, the earliest meeting of which had been held at Cambridge in the previous year, sprang suddenly, under the chairmanship of Bishop Wilberforce, into strong and mature life. But also a most remarkable debate took place, on that occasion, upon the broad subject which is now before us. That debate too, might, I think, be described by the same word "mature." I doubt whether, as regards general principles, much is likely to be said here to-day that was not in substance said in Oxford then.

Yet since that time great progress has been made, both in public opinion and in experiment. I may remind you that this same subject has been discussed, under various designations, in the Church Congresses of York, Dublin, and Stoke-upon-Trent, and that these meetings have been like stepping-stones across a period of anxious thought. It may, I think, be useful to glance at this progress, so as to see more distinctly where we stand at this moment.

(i.) First, there is the founding of the London Deaconess Institution, about that very same time, under the late Archbishop Tait, who (as was shown by a published letter from his deathbed) never relaxed his sympathetic hold on this subject. The foundation of other Deaconess Institutions has followed in the Dioceses of Ely, Canterbury, Chester, Salisbury, and in East London. Thus a large amount of experience has been gathered together, the pressure of difficulties has been felt, warnings have been supplied, and encouragement likewise.

(ii.) Another definite topic, on which stress must be laid, is this, that in 1871, under the presidency of the present Bishop of Winchester, a paper was drawn up, after very careful consultation, embodying certain principles and definitions, which were thought to meet the new demand for a Diaconate of Women, after the manner of early times, in the modern Church of England. From this paper I will simply quote the following:—(1.) "A Deaconess is a woman set apart by a Bishop, under that title, for service in the Church. (2.) No Deaconess or Deaconess Institution shall officially accept or resign work in a Diocese, without the express authority of the Bishop of that Diocese, which authority may at any time be withdrawn. (3.) No Deaconess shall officially accept work in a Parish (except it be in some Non-Parochial position, as in a Hospital, or the like), without the express authority of the Incumbent of that Parish, which authority may at any time be withdrawn. (4.) In all matters not connected with the parochial or other system, under which she is summoned to work, a Deaconess may, if belonging to a Deaconess Institution, act in harmony with the general rules of such Institution." On these definitions and this statement of principles I say nothing at present in the way of criticism. I will only add that the paper acquired importance from the signatures of nineteen of our Bishops; the two who have been removed by death, besides the Archbishop of Canterbury, being the Bishop of Saint David's, and the Bishop of Lichfield.

(iii.) This paper, however, obtained additional weight through the favourable manner of its reception in the same year by our Sister Church in America. I cannot help laying great stress on this fact, for religious ideas that take root in the United States are likely to have considerable influence on the future history of the world.

"Westward the course of Empire holds its way;"

and Bishop Berkeley's famous line certainly includes the empire of religious thought. It is enough to say that in that year a comprehensive report, "recognising," to use its own words, "the tested value of organisations of Christian women in prosecuting the work of Christ and His Church"—including, among other materials, the above-mentioned paper —and recommending the immediate adoption of practical measures, was presented to the General Convention of that year at Baltimore, and that from that year onward this general view of the place of authorised female ministrations in the Church has been widely accepted in America.

(iv.) Another circumstance which marks, not only a progress of public opinion during recent years, but a quickened activity of mind in this direction during the present year, is the fact that the subject has had a prominent place in the Diocesan Conferences of the Dioceses of Rochester, Peterborough, and Durham, while the correspondence and conversations which have surrounded these discussions show clearly that the question is widely viewed as very urgent.

(v.) But in this present year also our attention has been called, in connection with this question, to another occurrence across the Atlantic. In the Diocesan Synod of Montreal a canon has recently been adopted for the "setting apart by the Bishop of the Diocese of women of devout character and approved fitness for the work of a Deaconess." The details which follow are too long to quote; but they are very carefully drawn up, and they seem to me to be marked by practical good sense. Religious movements in the Colonies are by no means to be despised. It may hereafter be found that they react with much benefit on the Mother-Church at home.

(vi.) Nor in this slight survey of progress made during the last few years ought we to lose sight of another broad aspect of the subject. Our customary view of the general responsibilities, capabilities, and claims of women is not quite what it was in 1862. We recognise in them, more respectfully than we used to do, special capacities for service which could not be done equally well by men, and, co-ordinately with this, we recognise the duty of training them for such service. The establishment of schools for the higher education of women, the organising of the Girls' Friendly Society, the advancement made in the care of our hospitals and in provision for district-nursing, the removal of some prejudices regarding the dignity of remunerative employment for ladies who are not rich—these changes are indications of what I mean, and of what will be readily understood. The Deaconess question may in fact be said, under one point of view, to be the religious side of a much larger question, affecting, under the conditions of modern social life, what King Alfred called "the spindle side of the house."

The facts which have been enumerated are sufficient to show that this subject is pressing upon us with some weight, and that it rightfully demands our very careful attention. But now it seems proper to state more precisely what is intended by this word "Deaconess," what the thought is that underlies all this anxious desire for an organisation, which we do not possess at present except in a rudimentary form. Now the scheme, as it presents itself to me, is a very great and ambitious one. It is nothing less than an endeavour to restore to the Church what the Church has lost, what it was intended to have, what it did possess in the Primitive Age, and without which it is placed at a great disadvantage in the inevitable struggle against sin, ignorance, and sorrow. It seems to me that the modern state of society—with its separation of rich and poor, its intricate and delicate problems, its strain upon thought and feeling—needs quite as much as any previous age, perhaps more than any, an authorised and well-organised Ministry of Women.

It will be seen at once that this question is placed on strictly Church lines. It is a Church ministry, not a mere voluntary agency of any kind, which is demanded; and a great point is gained immediately by this mere statement of the case. All antagonism to anything else is put out of view. All opinions connected with other methods of female agency for religious and philanthropic ends remain just what they were before. The question ought to be viewed as having no entanglement with party, and as rising high above the mere fashion of the day. It is a Church question: and the Church will last longer than our parties and our fashions. Feminine agency may be crystallised into the exact form of sisterhoods, or may be diluted into the free movement of district visitors. These are not the precise inquiries before us. How much should be included under the Church Diaconate of Women, what varieties of method under one system should be allowed, is a question not of principle but of detail. What we want is the thing itself—an authorised official Diaconate of Women as an integral part of our Church system—a body of Deaconesses co-extensive with the Church itself, ready for service wherever they are needed—and the needs are very various—but appointed and directed by the Bishops, and serving under the Parochial Clergy.

But, moreover, the system which is here advocated

is on Bible lines as well as on Church lines: and, in fact, these two directions ought to be in strictest harmony with one another. It is an evil day when Church lines are not parallel with—or rather, I would say, not coincident with—Bible lines. Still there is this difference between the Ecclesiastical and the Scriptural aspects of such a subject, that the New Testament gives us principles rather than methods, whereas in practice we must arrange for definite methods. The Revised Version has rescued for us, out of most serious error, a clear statement of principle in this matter; and thus the publication of this version might most correctly have been named as one of the recent facts that have tended to bring this whole subject into prominence. Every one knows now, what was known to exact Biblical scholars before, that in the third chapter of St. Paul's First Epistle to Timothy, when the Apostle is describing the qualifications of those who are fit to be appointed to the lower and higher ministries of the Church, he describes the qualifications of women fit for their place in one part of such ministry. We need no longer perplex ourselves to find a reason why the wives of the Deacons should be admonished, whereas the wives of those who belong to a higher order receive none of that admonition which seems in their case to be equally requisite. We have in fact here in this eleventh verse the Man-Deacon and the Woman-Deacon co-ordinated side by side, in the same general ministry, just as we find to be the case afterwards in the post-apostolic age.

It has been remarked by the Bishop of Durham in his Primary Charge, that on Scriptural grounds Phœbe has quite as much right to be called a Deacon as has Stephen or Philip. But the case might with strict accuracy have been stated more strongly; for Stephen and Philip are nowhere designated by this term, whereas Phœbe is expressly so designated, while the nature of her work and her high responsibility are not obscurely indicated. It appears to me that if we take our stand simply on the ground of the New Testament, the argument for the recognition of Deaconesses as a part of the Christian Ministry is as strong as the argument for Episcopacy. And if anything approaching to this assertion is true, then two conclusions appear to follow: First, it is a daring responsibility to attempt to carry on the work of the Church without the acknowledgment of this principle, and we must expect to suffer if we make the attempt. Secondly, this mention of the ministerial appointment of women, where notices of the details of the Christian Ministry are so scanty, gives a new significance to the high honour paid to women, and to their prominent position, throughout the New Testament.

Of the Female Diaconate in the early ages after the time of the Apostles, I will only say this—and in a Diocese which contains a university it is worth while to say it—that the study of this subject deserves a closer attention than it has yet received. Such study, in fact, seems to be imperative: for surely it is probable that what was best for the primitive times is best for our own; and the Church of England has always professed to seek for precedents in the early ages. As to the special topics which such an inquiry includes, they are such as these—How were the Primitive Deaconesses appointed, and with what formalities? Did they ever live in community, or were they scattered and diffused, according to the exigencies that required them? What kind of work was assigned to them? In what relation did they stand to the Presbyterate and Episcopate? This list of questions might easily be augmented. But I will only add this remark on the point immediately before us, that I am persuaded that such research into the primitive facts relating to the women who were Deacons will be pursued to greater advantage if they are combined with inquiries into all that relates to Deacons of the other sex. Some modern mistakes on this latter subject are very likely to lead us astray. Our present Deacons are not the Deacons either of the Prayer-Book or of the Primitive Church.

We may, however, in that investigation of this whole subject which seems at present to be incumbent upon us, become too scholastic, too exclusively historical. The special experience, which is derived from the characteristics of our times, must be very carefully taken into account. And here it is to be noted that those women ought to be invited into council who have beeen actually doing work of this kind, while some of us have been speculating upon it. They may know much that we do not know. They may have observed many things which have escaped our notice. They may sometimes be better judges than we are of methods and details. Moreover, we must respectfully acknowledge their high devotion, and the claim they have established upon the gratitude of the Church. The woman's view of such a question as that which is before us cannot safely be neglected.

Yet there is another side of this part of our subject which must by no means be disregarded. Mere idle compliments, in such a discussion as this, would be impertinent and foolish. The best women are not always the wisest. Enthusiasm does not pause to calculate consequences: and the calculation of consequences is a serious duty in the handling of a delicate subject at a critical time. Mere preferences may be pushed to an extreme; and the responsibility of the harm which results may fall upon others, and involve them in the utmost difficulty.

> "How much of all that human hearts endure
> Women can rashly cause and cannot cure."

And another respectful appeal may, I hope, with propriety be made to our Bishops, that they take this subject into minute consideration, and manipulate it with a strong hand. It is of the essence of the very idea of the Deaconess system that it is not voluntary but official, and subject in all its parts to the knowledge and control of the Bishops. If a religious movement, associated with much zeal, is allowed to drift, it may assume harmful forms very difficult to correct. If usages grow up, and opinions become settled, which are out of harmony with our authorised standards of faith and practice, then peril to the Church must ensue. Above all, if esoteric understandings, not known to the Bishops, were to become secretly operative, that truthfulness, which is an essential part of holiness, would be, to say the least, in jeopardy. Even questions of costume and phraseology, in a matter of this kind, are of greater importance than at first sight appears.

In this paper I have endeavoured to limit myself to the statement of principles, avoiding mere details. Still there are two topics, which some might view as belonging to the region of detail, and some to the region of principle, and which I beg leave to name before I conclude.

The relation of Deaconess Institutions to Dioceses is not altogether a simple and easy question. I assume that Deaconess Institutions, more or less, must exist. Efficient training, both of religious character and in reference to future duties, is of the utmost moment. Moreover women, labouring in scattered places of work, often under very depressing circumstances, have need of a healthy bond of union to cheer them and strengthen them. Regarding the Deaconess Institutions of any one Diocese it is easy and obvious to say that it should be in all particulars—including, for instance, the books which are used in it—under the close and direct supervision of its own Bishop. But if a Deaconess, originally belonging to the Institution of one Diocese, is called to work in another Diocese, then some questions arise, which are not altogether free from difficulty. They are, in fact, parts of a larger question—viz. this, how, in the process of recovering the Diaconate of women, provision is to be made for a good understanding among different Dioceses, as to both principles and methods. As to the particular point which has led to this general remark, I will only add that though I regard the distributed work of Deaconesses in parishes as the main subject with which we have to do, yet to each such "servant of the Church" the possession of a home, to which she can return in case of failing health or great discouragement, is likely to be a treasure of great price.

The other topic, which I have reserved to the last, may be indicated under various forms of expression. Is this office of the Female Diaconate an office for life? Are such orders, if orders they are to be called, indelible? Are life-vows to be admitted, or to be required? And should such vows so far differ from the obligations of the Diaconate of Men, as to preclude the possibility of marriage? I purposely throughout this paper put the Diaconate of men and women side by side: for so they are placed, alike by St. Paul and in the records of the earlier Christian ages. As to the tenure of the office of a Deaconess, I certainly think that a woman presenting herself for the service ought to view it as a life-service. But the question of vows takes us to different ground. We cannot penetrate the secrets of any hearts, whether those secrets be wise or unwise. But as to official vows, given by authority, and revoked by authority, I confess I do not see where any power to this effect resides. I observe that Bishops are very reluctant to assume that they have any such power: and if any one less than a Bishop assumes that he has it, may it not be possible that he is deluded?

But, moreover, there remains the question whether such vows elevate the office or bring it down to a lower level. Here, however, I would rather use the words of another than my own. That question was definitely before us at that earlier meeting of the Church Congress in this Diocese: and Bishop Wilberforce, at the close of the meeting, said very seriously regarding vows of celibacy, made for life, or even for a limited period, that "as holding the office which God had given him, he could not take part in the arrangements of any institution in which such vows formed a part." He wished that there should be "no mistake" on this subject, and he gave three definite reasons as follows:—"First," he said, "I see no warrant for such vows in the Word of God; and it would seem to me that to encourage persons to make vows for which there is no distinct promise given that they should be able to keep them, would be entangling them in a yoke of danger. Secondly, it seems to me that our Church has certainly discouraged such vows. And, thirdly, it seems to me really to be of the essence of such a religious life that it should be continued, not because in a moment of past fervour a vow was made, but because by a continued life of love that life is again and again freely offered to that service to which it was definitely dedicated." He added that "instead of perpetual vows representing the higher, it was the admission of a lower standard;" and he said further, that "he had the deepest objection, in any way whatever, to apply the technical term 'religious' to such a life."

Those who were present on the occasion will remember the earnestness of tone with which these words were spoken. Nor is there any reason, so far as I am aware, for believing that Bishop Wilberforce ever changed his mind on the subject. Five years later he expressed the same opinion with equal strength. His memory will secure, from this audience at least, a respectful consideration of his deliberate utterance on this part of the subject: and incidents have not been wanting since, which add to what he then said the force of very grave experience.

THE CHURCH MINISTRY OF WOMEN.

A SPEECH IN CONVOCATION AT YORK ON JULY 16TH, 1884.

IN endeavouring to procure a favourable reception for the resolution which I am allowed to move, I will follow the order adopted in some remarks which I addressed to the Synod, in our last session, on the Extension of the Diaconate of Men. I will first refer to the authority which our subject derives from Holy Scripture and the Primitive Church; then, to the necessity which exists at this time for a revival of the Order of Deaconesses; and then I will allude to some objections to the whole matter, which may very naturally suggest themselves to the minds of some.

In itself I imagine this method is as convenient as any other: but there is a general reason for treating the Diaconate of Men and the Diaconate of Women in the same way, and presenting them to your notice as co-ordinate subjects. It is altogether within the limits of what may be termed the helping ministries of the Church that our discussion, on each occasion, has been and is restricted; and it is within those limits that the pressure of immediate need is most severely felt. I do not mean to say that a further subdivison of the Episcopate is not desirable; and we all know that a large reinforcement of the Presbyterate is urgently required. But our sorest need is a well-qualified helping ministry of various kinds; and I am quite persuaded that the Diaconate of Men and the Diaconate of Women will be considered by us to the greatest advantage, if we place them side by side, and if inquiries into them are conducted co-ordinately—not necessarily by the same persons or according to the same methods, but under the conviction that they are parts of one subject. At our last meeting we tried our 'prentice hand on the Diaconate of Men; we have now to deal with the more difficult and delicate question of the Diaconate of Women.

It is in this combination with the Diaconate of Men that the Diaconate of Women is brought before us in that 3rd chapter of the First Epistle to Timothy, to which our minds inevitably turn when we begin to think of the Biblical aspect of this question—"Even so must the woman-deacons be grave, not slanderers, sober, faithful in all things." I desire to put this Biblical aspect of the question before the Synod in a very pointed manner; but, though I may cause some surprise, I shall simply say what I believe to be the bare and literal truth. It seems to me that, as to Bible authority for Women-Deacons among the ministries of the Church, the case for them is stronger than for the existence of Bishops. I am perfectly loyal to the Episcopate. I am not a Presbyterian or a Quaker in disguise. But how does the word "bishop" appear before us in the New Testament? St. Paul sends for the Elders of Ephesus to meet him at Miletus; and when they come, he calls them Bishops. He tells Titus that he placed him in Crete that he might ordain Elders in every city, and when he proceeds to describe their qualifications, he calls them Bishops. It is difficult, on the theory of any other use of words, to explain the opening of the Epistle to the Philippians, or the omission of all allusion to Presbyters in that chapter of the First Epistle to Timothy to which I first referred.

THE CHURCH MINISTRY OF WOMEN. 45

But the Deaconesses are set before us in two epistles, of very different dates, with perfect distinctness. Or let us look at the matter in another way. No Bishop, no Presbyter, in the New Testament is spoken of individually by name. Who the "elders" were that received the earliest alms at Jerusalem, who the "bishops" were, that were ordained for service at Ephesus, in Crete and at Philippi, we know not. Even with regard to the Deacons no person whose name is given is called a "deacon." But we have the honoured name of a deaconess of a suburb of Corinth, clearly given. As we look back into these dim annals of the earliest Christian communities, we see there the figure of Phœbe, as the solitary one who is named; and something is told to us likewise of her character and of her work. It is right, I think, that she should be viewed as the type of a large amount of special service in the Church of Christ, which would be a blessing to mankind.

But it is essential that we look also at the period which immediately succeeded the time of the New Testament: and there we see as clearly as possible the Man-Deacon and the Woman-Deacon side by side. In Pliny's well-known letter women are the only ministers who are specified. But it is the combination of the two sides of the Diaconate on which I lay chief stress: and, as to this point, I will simply refer to that remarkable collection of documents known as the Apostolical Constitutions. To what dates their different parts belong is of no moment to my argument. I imagine no part of them belongs to a period as late as that of Chrysostom, Jerome, and Augustine: and if they came together gradually during the earliest ages of the Church, as probably they did, this adds great force to the mention of Deaconesses which we find there, and to that co-ordination of which I have spoken. The facts of the case can easily be tested by any one in a very short time. I have casually mentioned Chrysostom. Both his Church-work at Constantinople and the circumstances of his personal life make manifest to us the very large place then filled by Deaconesses: but there is another part of this primitive aspect of the question to which special attention should be given.

I refer to what I may term the Liturgical side of the subject. If a Ministry of the Church appears, not only floating about, so to speak, in the earlier

THE CHURCH MINISTRY OF WOMEN. 47

Christian literature, but embodied in Church Services, then it surely exerts a new claim upon our inquiry. Now not only is there in the Apostolic Constitutions a prescribed prayer for the setting apart of Deaconesses, but in one section of the Eastern Church we find a distinct service for setting them apart; while in another section we find, in the service for the Consecration of Bishops, a prayer for the Divine blessing on his "creation" of "Presbyters, Deacons and Deaconesses." And it is to be added, while we are touching the Liturgical side of our subject, that Deaconesses appear to have been sometimes employed, as assistant ministers, in the actual administration of the consecrated elements to female communicants. We are reminded here, at another point, of a correlative topic, namely, the need expressed at our last meeting of the help of Deacons during this service.

This is of course a very small part of a large subject: but there is no time for more under this head. Inquiries are in progress among eminent theologians for fuller information regarding the Primitive Diaconate of Women. But surely enough has been said under this point of view to show that we have before us a very serious subject. If we act in continued disregard of the practice of the early Church in this respect, and persist in denuding our e clesiastical system of any official ministry of women, it is probable that we shall suffer, and that those who come after us will suffer too.

I come, then, to our necessity in this matter: and first I would remark that we have here the religious side of a general "woman's question," which is pressing upon us with extreme urgency at this time. We are living in the midst of a kind of revolution, on what, I believe, King Alfred used to call "the spindle side of the house:" and, on the whole, I believe it to be a most healthy and most Christian revolution. No doubt we have folly here and extravagance to encounter. There is almost always a fringe of folly and extravagance in connection with every new social movement, even if on the whole it is a wise movement. I allude now to the change which has taken place in public opinion in regard to the remunerative work of women, to their larger independence within the limits of strict decorum, to their powerful beneficial service in hospitals, and in schools of a new type.

But let us think of this necessity of a Diaconate

of Women in its deeper meaning. We who are assembled here to-day in this Metropolitan city of the Northern province, travelled yesterday along various lines through a district of no great extent, which yet contains more of the hopes and fears of the future for mankind than any other region of similar extent in the world. We came from Newcastle and Durham, from Liverpool and Manchester, from Wakefield and Sheffield, from Chester, from Carlisle: and what did we see as we travelled? We saw great railway stations in progress. The characteristic architecture around us consisted of tall chimneys. What did we feel to be the great need of the Clergy, who are at work, in numbers far too scanty, in these places? They want Deacons: and I hope they will obtain them. But there is one thing they need far more urgently. They need among their people the living presence of well-educated refined Christian women, capable of helping the poor wisely, and well trained in the management of the sick, working under parochial rule and in connection with other parochial efforts. Even if the Clergy were in sufficient numbers, yet, however zealous they may be, there are many things which they cannot do, and which require for the doing of them, the gentle touch, the ready wit, the domestic sympathy of women. And many women there are ready to devote themselves actively, tenderly, patiently in this way. But for the most part the workers are in one place and the work is in another. And let us not forget that we are all living under extreme pressure, with nerves overwrought, with sensibilities excited, and with peculiar liability to sin and misery on this account. Whatever the needs of the Primitive Church were in this matter, our own needs are more urgent.

If such is the necessity which presses upon us, if the general character of the remedy for a widely-spread malady can be so easily prescribed, we should surely neglect our duty in this assembly if we were to continue to disregard this subject, and refuse to give to it our close and patient attention.

But now I turn to objections—of course there are objections—and their very existence renders this close and patient attention the more imperative. I will limit myself to three topics of this kind; and first, there is a dread in some minds lest harm should come through women living in community. It is feared that if a system of Deaconesses be established among us, there may be a recurrence of those evils, which, as we all know, have existed aforetime in connection with communities of women. Let me then say, speaking from my own point of view, that I regard the Deaconess Institution as a means to an end, or rather as a means to more ends than one. It is not of the essence of the office of a Deaconess, but it is an important element in securing her efficiency. It is a place for training; and it is a home which may be a refuge and solace in time of sickness and discouragement, and which may tend to bind together the Deaconesses of a Diocese in sympathy and mutual help. Of course we cannot limit the freedom of our Bishops as to those women whom they should set apart for the Deaconess office. Some of the fittest women may be those who have never been connected with any institution at all. Moreover, all Dioceses are not alike in their conditions and their necessities. But an institution is of the utmost value for the gathering up and storing up of experience. And let me add two remarks, each of which seems to me of the greatest importance. I see on all sides a desire for capable district nurses, for parochial mission-women of a higher social rank than heretofore, and the like: and it seems to be thought enough to plant such workers for the poor in solitary lodgings in gloomy streets. Now this appears to me to be cruelty. Work of this kind is conducted under the most depressing circumstances, often with great fatigue, in the midst of suffering, squalor, and sin: and to condemn a woman of sensitive nature, who has worked in this way through the day, and perhaps through the night, to so dreary a home, is bad policy, and implies lack of sympathy. But, on the other hand, I must urge with equal force, that everything connected with such institutions, including the books of devotion that are used, and the customary phraseology that is adopted, ought unequivocally to be within the knowledge and under the control of the Bishop. If, for instance, while certain outward rules are under his cognisance and approval, some esoteric rules were withheld from him, this would seem to me, not only to involve great risks, but to be out of harmony with our old-fashioned English notions of fairness and truth.

Another objection is connected with the question

of indelibility of orders. If Deaconesses are officially admitted among the orders of Church ministries, it will naturally be asked how this question affects them. On this I shall say but little, for I regard it as part of a larger subject which deserves very careful study. It was before our minds recently, when we were considering the Extension of the Diaconate of Men. We are somewhat in the habit of assuming points of theology, which have been handed on from book to book, and even to become very hot about them, without examining the foundations upon which they rest. Among these subjects is, I suspect, the question of indelibility, as regards the Diaconate both of Men and Women. Inquiries, as I have said, are in progress regarding the history and organisation of the Deaconess system in early ages; and I find it stated by learned men of our day, of different schools of thought, that our customary Western view of this question of indelibility has not precisely a counterpart in the theological opinion of the Eastern Church. This subject, I imagine, demands more study than has hitherto been given to it. Meantime, however, I venture to say confidently that Deaconess work, deliberately undertaken, ought to be viewed as a life-work, and not as a mere transient occupation to be laid aside at will.

We are thus inevitably brought, under the head of objections, to the question which is the most delicate of all—the question of Vows. It is essential that we clear our minds as to what in this case we mean by vows. There is much confusion of thought on this subject. We do not mean, in this instance, a life-pledge as to property or a life-pledge as to obedience. I do not imagine that any one proposes that when a woman is made a Deaconess she should resign all her property, or promise to obey any one absolutely in all things, even though he be a Bishop. What we mean is really a life-pledge of celibacy. Now this is a very serious matter indeed; and I hope this Synod will bear with me in what I am about to say. We of the Clergy are very willing to set aside the widely-diffused sentiment of the Early Church in favour of Clerical Celibacy, and we allow to ourselves a very large freedom as regards marriage; and, as a consequence, our homes are very happy. Is it altogether generous if we peremptorily decide the question the other way for women appointed to a ministerial office in the Church? I will not myself dogmatise on the subject of vows. I would rather content myself with referring to utterances of four of our Bishops, each one of whom deserves our respectful attention. The first is Bishop Wilberforce, who was in the chair at the Oxford Church Congress, when the discussion of this whole subject sprang, in a most remarkable manner, to a sudden maturity. Dr. Pusey, on that occasion, spoke strongly in favour of vows. The chairman took a different view, and expressed this difference of view with a most earnest solemnity. No one, who was present at the meeting, can forget how, at the close of it, he warned us against the perils of such vows, and told us that free, loving service, rendered day by day, was a far higher and nobler thing than service rendered because of a promise which was made years before, and which allows of no escape. Next I may refer to a meeting which took place at Ely House, in Dover Street, when the present Bishop of Winchester was Bishop of Ely. On that occasion the present Bishop of Salisbury said that, whatever opinions might be held regarding vows of this kind, he knew of no power which had been given to him to impose them or release from them.

Another Prelate, who is still with us for our example and instruction, is the Bishop of Lincoln. He published a few years ago a letter addressed to Sir George Prevost, in which he warned us very seriously of the risks involved in pledges of this kind. And now I must quote another revered Bishop, whose voice comes to us literally from the chamber of death: for our dear and honoured Bishop Jacobson passed away from this life the day before yesterday, and he is to be laid in his grave the day after to-morrow. He gave not only his personal sanction, but his warmest encouragement to our successful efforts to promote Deaconess work in Chester; and the words at the close of his opening speech, when we began this work in 1867, were these: After quoting the maxim of the Reformers that "the abuse of a thing doth not take away the lawful use of it," he proceeds—"It matters not to me whether such women work singly and individually, or in concert and association more or less formal. What I do bargain for in giving my formal sympathy and official support to the movement is, that there shall be nothing whatever required in the shape of vows; and as a matter of advice, I would

THE CHURCH MINISTRY

venture to add that there ought to b
of mediæval peculiarities—no adoption
likely to give offence, and to do little ⸺
cause their good to be evil spoken of." T
high authorities I will add nothing on my own p
except just to say this, that we have at this moment
around us very grave dangers of this kind, and that
the Bishops cannot with safety to the Church disregard them. Thus I have heard of young women, on taking vows of this nature, being separately married to our Lord Jesus Christ with orange blossoms, a bridal dress, and a wedding ring. It seems to me, that this is utterly inconsistent with reverence, and an unwholesome indulgence of that side of the female character which needs control rather than encouragement. Moreover, I must confess that I am very sensitive as to making ourselves ridiculous, by such imitations, in the eyes of members of the great modern Church of Rome, with whose system such things are as congenial as they are alien from our own.

What I have laid before the Synod is a general statement of principles, to the best of my ability, and what I ask for is a general approbation of those

ne resolution will be seconded by
Gore, who has long been familiar with
t, and who has given to this good cause
areful thought and active work. If the re-
ion is accepted, I hope a committee will be
appointed for careful inquiry and practical suggestions. Meantime, our discussion here may do much towards the formation of public opinion. It is this action upon public opinion which constitutes a large part of our responsibility on these occasions—the responsibility, on the one hand, for addressing ourselves with courage to grave and urgent questions, and responsibility, on the other hand, for praying that our words may be Divinely guided so as to be words of prudence and wisdom.

THE PRIMITIVE DIACONATE OF WOMEN.

BEING APPENDIX I. OF THE REPORT ON THE CHURCH MINISTRY OF WOMEN, PRESENTED TO CONVOCATION AT YORK, ON THE 22D OF APRIL, 1885.

I HAVE been requested to prepare some historical notes on this work in its Primitive form. It appears to me that the best mode of doing this is to state what has been done in this direction at the instance of certain meetings recently held in London, and then to add such conclusions, or at least opinions, as I have been able to reach.

These meetings were held for the discussion of the whole question of "Deaconesses," last year, on the 19th of June and the 7th of November, at the Palace, Lambeth, and in the Jerusalem Chamber, Westminster. Among those present with us were the ARCHBISHOP OF CANTERBURY, the BISHOPS OF WINCHESTER, BATH AND WELLS, LICHFIELD AND

BEDFORD, and a considerable number of Clergy of high character and large experience.

In the course of discussion it was felt that more information was needed respecting the history, the work, and the regulations of the Primitive Diaconate of Women: and the ARCHDEACONS OF CHESTER AND MACCLESFIELD with myself were requested to draw up a paper of questions to be submitted to carefully chosen men of recognised theological learning—the questions having reference to topics which came prominently to view during these meetings.

The following is the paper of questions drawn up in pursuance of these arrangements:

DEACONESSES IN THE PRIMITIVE CHURCH.

1.—THE LAYING ON OF HANDS.—(a) Was this customary, or viewed as essential, in the appointment of Deaconesses? (b) Was the laying on of hands viewed as conveying an indelible character?

2. AGE.—(a) What were considered in Primitive times to be the fitting limits of age within which a Deaconess should be set apart? (b) How far did regulations as to this point vary from time to time, or in different parts of the Church?

3. MARRIAGE.—(a) Were married women, as distinct from widows, ever set apart as Deaconesses? (b) Were women who were set apart as Deaconesses ever allowed to marry afterwards without resigning their office?

4. VOWS.—(a) On the admission of Deaconesses were vows exacted? If not, were they permitted? If there were such vows, what did they include as to property, celibacy, &c.? (b) Were vows for a limited time ever sanctioned? (c) If there were vows, with whom rested the power of imposing them or releasing from them?

5. COMMUNITIES.—How far does it appear that Deaconesses were banded together in communities, or that they worked freely in separate places according to the needs that might arise?

6. TRAINING.—To what training and probation were they subjected before being admitted?

7. DISCONTINUANCE OF THE ORDER.—What light can you throw on the circumstances which led to the disappearance of Deaconesses from the Western Church?

8. AUTHORITIES.—Can you furnish us with a list of authorities on this general subject, which it would be useful to consult?

April 2, 1884.

The best method to adopt, in giving the substance of the answers which have been received, will be to follow the order of the questions: and, inasmuch as the correspondents, who have written most fully, have been Dr. BRIGHT, Regius Professor of Ecclesiastical History in Oxford, Dr. STOKES, Professor of Ecclesiastical History in Dublin, Dr. LITTLEDALE, ARCHDEACON NORRIS, Dr. REICHEL, Dean of Clonmacnoise,[1] and the Rev. E. KNOWLES, Principal of St. Bees' College, the following abbreviations will be used—B., S., L., N., R., K.

1. THE LAYING ON OF HANDS.—(a) "Prescribed in the Apostolical Constitutions (viii.–19), implied by St. Basil (Ep. 199–44) and practised in 5th century (C. of Chalcedon, Can. 15). See also the Constantinopolitan rite of ordaining them (Goar's Euchologium, p. 262). The interpretation of Can. 19 of the C. of Nicæa is doubtful: perhaps the best way is to take it as meaning that the Deaconesses of the Paulicianist heresy were not ordained by the laying on of hands. Sozomen (8–9) says that Nectarius ἐχειροτόνησε Olympias. But Western Councils from A.D. 441 onwards forbade any more Deaconesses to be *ordained*: and even in the East the Laodicean Council had forbidden the appointment of any more elderly women, probably chief Deaconesses."—B. After reference to the same authorities and with the same view regarding the Deaconesses of the sect of Paul of Samosata (ἐπεὶ μηδὲ χειροθεσίαν τίνα ἔχουσιν) "the Montanists according to Hilary (Ambrosiastes) ordained Dea-

[1] Now Bishop of Meath.

conesses." This would throw the practice back to Cent. ii. Cf. Concil. Laod., Can. xi. (about A.D. 350) and Epiph. Hær. 79–4. The nature of such χειρο-θεσία has been a question much disputed by Valesius, Van Espen, Baronius, Justellus, Morinus, Neander, Hefele. It would seem by the decision of the Council of Orange (A.D. 441) that it was commonly regarded as a true Ordination and not merely as an act of Benediction. That council decided as follows—" Diaconissæ omnimodis non ordinandæ: si quæ jam sunt, benedictioni quæ populo impenditur capita submittant."—S. "The Apost. Const. attest the practice of laying on of hands at the end of the third century and probably the tradition of the second. Paulicianist Deaconesses were not so ordained by laying on of hands. Catholic ones were so ordained, and reckoned among the Clergy."—L. "I have always concluded from the Canons of Nicæa and Chalcedon that Deaconesses had not any imposition of hands. If some passages seem to imply that they had, it must be due to the early confusion of the words χειροτονεῖν and χειροθετεῖν."—N. "In Goar there is a regular service for the ordination of Deaconesses, conducted exactly on the lines of the ordination of a Deacon. Whatever prerogatives he had she enjoyed."—R.

(*b*) "As the office was not *in sacris* but *circa sacra*, it is inconceivable that the idea of indelible character could attach to it."—B. "Indelibility would seem to follow from what is said by the C. of Chalcedon and in the law of Justinian."—S. "This theory of χαρακτήρ, however implicitly it may be involved in early teaching on Holy Orders, is legally a scholastic development of a comparatively late age; and no assertion can be safely made on the subject, in view of the facility and frequency of deposition in the Early Church."—L. "It was indelible."—N. "In the ancient Greek Services I find no trace of the indelibility of orders."—R. "There has been, I think, no definition of the indelible character of orders in the Eastern Church. Such a term is avoided by her theologians, who, however, practically infer the doctrine from the Apostolic Canon."—K.

2. AGE—(*a, b*) "The old limit of age was ordinarily such as to exclude very young women. Tertullian, referring, it seems, to Deaconesses under the name of widows who had been but once married,

speaks after St. Paul's rule, of the age of 60 (de Vel. Virg. 9). But the C. of Chalcedon (c. 15) lowers this to 40; and Olympias was but newly a widow when made a Deaconess. The Church varied the rule as in the case of Ordination."—B. "The Emperor Theodosius (A.D. 390) passed a law that no woman should be admitted to this order save such as were 60 years of age and had had children (Sozom. H. E. vii. 16, and Cod. Theod. Tit. de Epise. lex. 27). Forty seems to have been the age from A.D. 451."—S. "Can. xv. of Chalcedon was re-enacted by the Council in Trullo. I think that if an earlier age had previously been admitted, the Council would have said so; for the tendency in cases of this sort is usually towards relaxation, not towards stringency. Justinian (Novell.) and Photius both name 50 years, thus showing that the Laodicean Canon had not been taken as fully binding in the East."—L. "Tertullian probably misunderstood St. Paul."—N.

3. MARRIAGE.—(a) "I know of no case of a married woman, whose husband was still alive (*i.e.*, who was living as a married woman), being made Deaconess. The Apost. Const. and Epiphanius

speak as if Deaconesses must be either virgins or widows who had but once married.—B. "From the time of Polycarp and the Pastoral Epistles matrimony and the office of a deaconess were regarded as inconsistent with one another."—S. "Only widows, or the widow of one single husband were eligible. (See Apost. Const. vi. 17, Just. Novell. cxxii. 13)."—L. "Sometimes in Provincial Canons the term 'Deaconess' is applied to wives of Deacons; but this is clearly a misuse of the term."—N.

(*b*) "The 15th C. of Chalcedon anathematises a Deaconess who disposes of herself in marriage and thus 'does despite to the grace of God.' St. Basil (Epist. 199, 24) said that the widow enrolled among the widows (*i.e.*, the widow serving as a Deaconess) had been put under censure by St. Paul if she married."—B. "I do not think they were allowed to marry at all, save under the heaviest ecclesiastical and temporal penalties (Cf. 2d C. of Orleans, c. 17, 18, A.D. 533.) These Canons seem to view the marriage as null and void, since the Deaconess was encouraged to break it."—S. "No trace whatever of married Deaconesses."—L.

4. Vows.—(*a, b, c*) "That which was spoken of by

St. Paul as violated by a Church widow who married would be *like* a vow. Deaconesses probably made such a vow, not necessarily in formal terms, but as a promise. These promises, however, would not relate to property. Olympias retained her property. The power of imposing and releasing would naturally be the Bishop."—B. "Ordination by imposition of hands implies vows of some kind. Celibacy was certainly included. The 11th c. of the 4th C. of Carthage (A.D. 398) runs thus:—'If a virgin is to be presented to the Bishop for consecration, it must be in the same clothes which in accordance with her sacred calling she will hereafter wear.' In Cyprian (Ep. iv.) we find the Bishop dispensing with the vows of such virgins as found matrimony a physical necessity."—S. "There are no vows in the Greek Ordinal for Deaconesses, which is perhaps the earliest evidence extant. Dispensations from vows do not appear, so far as I know, in the East at all; and in the West they are not earlier than the twelfth century, so far as I know."—L. "I do not find in the ancient Ordination Offices any trace of vows, either of celibacy or of obedience."—R.[1]

[1] It is important to call attention to what is said by Canon Body in his part of this Appendix to the Convocation Report:—"We

68   THE PRIMITIVE DIACONATE OF WOMEN.

5. COMMUNITIES.—"There was no reason in the nature of their office for a community life. They worked freely as might best suit the needs that might arise. The two Deaconesses (Ministræ) whom Pliny put to the torture were maid-servants (ancillæ.) Virgins, however, who were also Deaconesses, might, in some cases, live in community. This seems to have been the case with Lampadia: and the widow-Deaconess Olympias appears to have superintended a community of young women."—B. "Both systems seem to have prevailed: for we find Justinian (Novell. 6) ordaining that if Deaconesses are ordained younger than the appointed age of fifty or forty, they shall enter a monastery. Those ordained at the accustomed age are to live along with their fathers, brothers, or sons. I should conclude that the majority of Deaconesses were attached to separate churches."—S. "The most trustworthy evidence shows a large number of Deaconesses grouped about

<small>have no reason to believe that vows were ever made by women on entering on this life in the Primitive Church. What bound them to their life was that solemn consecration to it they had sought and received through the Church. Whether vows are used as the condition of that consecration or not is a question of expediency. . . . The obligations of the dedicated life can be dispensed; for consecration to it confers no *character*."</small>

great churches, such as that of St. Sophia at Constantinople. Possibly some did missionary work in heathen households singly, like the Zenana mission-women in modern times."—L.

6. TRAINING.—"The C. of Chalcedon (c. 15) requires 'accurate probation,' doubtless as to moral character, fitness for instructing women-catechumens, stability of purpose, &c."—B. "The 4th C. of Carthage (c. 12) implies some kind of testing and training."—S.

7. DISCONTINUANCE OF THE ORDER.—"The Laodicean prohibition in the Eastern Church is explained by Hefele to refer probably to some over-stepping of the limits of their office by these Senior Deaconesses: and this reason may be thought to have prompted some of the Western Councils to suppress the Order. The second C. of Orleans (A.D. 533) gives another reason, viz., 'pro conditionis hujus fragilitate,' apparently referring to 1 Tim. v. 11. See Mansi, Concil. S. 837."—B. "I should think it was the frequency of the marriage of Deaconesses, and the increasing veneration for celibacy in the 6th cent., which caused their abolition."—S. "The terms of the abrogating Canon seem to point to scandals. The security of the

cloister may have been thought essential in that rough age."—L.

[To these remarks by others, to whom the utmost gratitude is due, I add, in the simplest form, the following remarks of my own:—

(1.) The diversity of opinion, which exists now even among learned men, regarding some parts of this general subject, shows that such parts ought to receive renewed and very careful attention.

(2.) As to the "Indelibility of Orders" in the case of both Deacons and Deaconesses I suspect that the traditional views of Anglican Theologians may admit of reconsideration.

The following passage in the "Life and Correspondence of Dr. Arnold" is by no means yet obsolete, and the plea which he makes there is as forcible as ever:—

"A great point might be gained by urging the restoration of the Order of Deacons, which has been long, quoad the reality, dead. In large towns many worthy men might be found able and willing to undertake the office out of pure love, if it were understood to be not necessarily a step to the Presbyterial Order, nor at all incompatible with lay callings. . . . . The Canon Law, I think, makes a very wide distinction between the Deacon and the Presbyter. The Deacon, according to it, is half a layman, and could return at any time to a lay condition altogether; and I suppose no one is so mad as to maintain that a minister abstaining from all secular callings is a matter of necessity, seeing that St. Paul carried on his trade of tent-maker even when he was an Apostle. Of course the ordination service might remain just as it is; for in fact no alteration in the law is needed;—it is only an alteration in certain customs which have long prevailed but which have really no authority. It would be worth while, I think, to consult the Canon Law and our own Ecclesiastical Law, so far as we have any, with regard to the Order of Deacons."—Vol. II., pp. 149, 150.

(3.) In the early ages I imagine that the laying on of hands was larger and more vague in its scope than is customary in our present view. Mr. Maskell, in his "Monumenta Ritualia," distinctly expresses the opinion that the setting apart of Deaconesses in this way was an act rather of benediction than of ordination.

The following passage is found at page xcv. of Volume III. of the edition of his "Monumenta Ritualia Ecclestiæ Anglicanæ," which he published before he joined the Church of Rome. In the second edition which he published after becoming a Roman Catholic, the page is cvii. of Vol. II.

"Some have argued that in the first centuries women were ordained, and appealed to the 'Presbyteræ' and 'Episcopæ' whom we meet with in many records. But these were the wives of priests and bishops, either before or after their ordination . . . Nor can the Deaconesses of the primitive ages be taken as any precedent for such a custom; for independently of their functions being strictly kept separate from any matter appertaining to the priesthood, or to the public service of the Church, and being limited to the performance of mere secular duties, such as visiting the sick, and catechising women, &c., it is very doubtful whether they received imposition of hands . . . Even if after all there may seem to be a balance of evidence in favour of some imposition of hands, yet this was in the way of a Benediction and not of Ordination."

Here I think Mr. Maskell takes too restricted

a view of the official religious duties of Primitive Deaconesses. Even "catechising" is far from a secular employment. As to the decree of the Council of Nice, which has caused so much difficulty, I am convinced that when it is said that these women had never received benediction by the laying on of hands, it is not meant that hands had not been laid upon them, but that Heresy had put them outside of the reality of Christian ordinances. The imposition of hands in their case had not been a true ecclesiastical consecration. See the remarks on Deaconesses in Canon Bright's learned book on "the Canons of the First Four General Councils," pp. 69, 171.

(4.) The late Bishop of Lincoln, in a pamphlet which he published on "Sisterhoods and Vows" a few years before his death, wrote as follows:—"The terms *Sister* and *Sisterhood*, as now used in the Church of England, do not correspond to anything known to the Christian Church for 1000 years . . . The word *Sisterhood* has no correlative in the terminology of the ancient Greek or Latin Church. It is unknown to both; it would not be possible to translate it by any word used by either. The ancient Church had its *Widows*, it had its *Virgins*, it had its

Deaconesses; it had *no Sisterhoods* in the modern sense of the term."—Letter to the Venerable Sir George Prevost, Bart., pp. 13, 14.

This mention of *Widows* calls to mind a very important observation made by the Bishop of Durham in Convocation at York. He stated expressly that he had been brought to the conclusion that the *Widows* and *Deaconesses* named by St. Paul were from the first two different kinds of feminine ministration. The expression of this opinion he has recently renewed in his great work on the Epistles of Ignatius. The phrase which gives occasion to this criticism is that in which Ignatius writes to the Smyrnæans, "I salute the Virgins who are called Widows." On the one hand Bishop Lightfoot says, "From their mention in this salutation as distinct from the households of the brethren with their wives and children, it is clear they were persons who lived apart from the family life of the rest:" on the other hand he says, "The interpretation of the language of Ignatius has been confused by the assumption that the Widows were the same Order as the Deaconesses. This, however, seems to be quite a mistake. Whatever confusion there may have been in later times, in the Apostolic age, and for some generations after Ignatius, they were distinct."—Vol. II., s. i., pp. 322, 323.

(5.) Bishop Charles Wordsworth, in his pamphlet on "Sisterhoods and Vows," wrote most truly. "The subject is one of much importance and intricacy: it demands careful consideration and study, and requires that statements with respect to it should be made with caution, clearness, and accuracy." In illustration of the difference between a vow and a promise he refers to Bishop Sanderson.[1]

(6.) As to the alleged abolition of the office of Deaconess, I doubt whether correct language is always used on this subject. Decisions of Local Councils would not necessarily affect the Church at large. I find prayers at the making of Deaconesses

---

[1] See Bishop Jacobson's edition, 1864. In Vol. IV. are seven Prælections "de juramenti obligatione," and in Vol. V. Bishop Sanderson illustrates "the case of a rash vow deliberately iterated." On the whole it appears to me that there may be less theoretical and practical difficulty in this matter than has often been imagined. A vow made to God is one thing, a promise made to man is another. That which is to be deprecated is the entangling of the consciences of women by those who have never received any Church authority to do this.

in the York Pontificals of Egbert (A.D. 732) and of Bainbridge (A.D. 1508), both published by the Surtees Society.

In the former (p. 94), the "Benedictio Episcopalis in Ordinatione Diaconissæ" is given in precisely the same manner, and in strict parallelism with the same benediction as "in Ordinatione Diaconi." In the former case the Bishop prays that the Almighty God, "qui de antiquo hoste etiam per feminas voluit triumphare," will vouchsafe to bless the women thus ordained. In the latter case he prays that the Deacons ordained may be blessed by the God who is "misericordia plenus, pietate immensus, majestate gloriosus, uirtute pracipuus." In the latter volume, the prayer in question is found in an appendix containing extracts from the pontifical of Leofric, Bishop, first of Crediton, and then of Exeter, in the tenth century. The prayer "ad Diaconissam faciendam" is as follows: Exaudi, Domine, preces nostras, et super hanc famulam tuam *ill*. Spiritum tuæ benedictionis emitte, ut cælesti munere ditata, et tuæ gratiam possit majestatis acquirere et bene vivendi aliis exemplum præbere," 342. It is surely made evident by these passages that at these dates Bishops had the power of appointing and setting apart Deaconesses whensoever they pleased.]

8. AUTHORITIES.—If I could have fulfilled my promise thoroughly, I should have concluded with a large list of books which bear directly or indirectly upon this subject of the Primitive Diaconate of Women. Under present circumstances I will limit myself to the mention of the following: [1]—

> 1.—Ziegler: "De Diaconis et Diaconissis." — Wittenberg, 1678.
>
> 2.—The late Bishop of Lincoln's Notes, in his Greek Testament, on the following passages : 1 Tim. iii. 11, v. 3.
>
> 3.—Bingham's "Antiquities of the Christian Church."— Book II. ch. xxii., and VII. ch. x.
>
> 4.—Various Essays in German and English, published at Kaiserwerth, especially by Pastor Fliedner.
>
> 5.—"Six Months among the Charities of Europe," by John de Liedfe (2 Vols., London, 1865).
>
> 6.—"Sisterhoods and Deaconesses at Home and Abroad," by the Rev. H. C. Potter, C.D. (now Coadjutor Bishop of New York.)—New York, 1873.

---

[1] I attach great importance to what is said by M. Renan on this subject. On the one hand he is free from partisanship on such a point, and on the other hand he retains much of his old ecclesiastical sympathies. His historical insight enables him to perceive in the institutions of the very earliest Church both the marvellous appearance of the ministry of women as a great fact, and the official appointment of women-deacons side by side with the men-deacons.

It should be very carefully noticed that the indirect evidence furnished by Liturgical Services constitutes an evidence more cogent than any evidence which is direct.[1] The learned writers quoted above have referred to what is found of this kind in the work of Goar. I may be allowed to add what I produced in the preface to my work on "Deaconesses," from Assemanni—viz., a distinct "Ordo Chirotoniæ Mulierum Diaconissarum," parallel for the most part to the similar service for the appointment of Deacons. It is fair and right that I should add that the following Rubric is found in this service:—" Imponit Episcopus Manum Super Caput ejus, non per modum Chirotoniæ, sed Benedictionem ei imperitur, et recitat super illam precationem secretam pro viribus suis."

Nothing is more important, on this side of the subject, than a careful study of it in the "Apostolical Constitutions." And no evidence there of the widely-spread existence of the system of Deaconesses among the ministries of the Church is of greater force than the fact that the following prayer was in use:—

---

[1] More on this subject will be found in the volume of Daniel's "Codex Liturgicus," which relates to ordination.

"Eternal God, Father of our Lord Jesus Christ, Creator both of man and woman, who didst fill with Thy Holy Spirit Mary, Deborah, Anna, and Huldah,—who didst not disdain that Thy Only Begotten Son should be born of a woman, who also in the Tabernacle of Testimony and in the Temple didst appoint women as the keepers of Thy holy gates; look now Thyself on this Thine handmaid, here set apart for the office of a Deaconess; give unto her Thy Holy Spirit, cleanse her from all impurity of the flesh and of the spirit, that she may worthily accomplish the task now committed unto her, to Thy glory and the praise of Thy Christ, with Whom to Thee and the Holy Spirit be glory and worship for ever and ever. Amen."

SPEECH,

IN CONVOCATION AT YORK, APRIL 23D, 1885, ON PRESENTING THE REPORT ON THE CHURCH MINISTRY OF WOMEN, ETC., ETC.

THE culmination of this subject in Convocation at York last April was of so important and encouraging a character, so much pains were taken in the preparation of the report directed to be prepared after the debate of 1884, the debate in the present year on the presentation of the report was so serious and complete, and the resolution finally adopted so satisfactory, that I am tempted to reprint in a separate form the speech which I made on presenting the report.

The motion which I originally brought forward was of a very simple kind, to the following effect: "That a ministry of women, in general harmony with the system of Deaconesses in the Primitive Church, and adapted to the requirements of modern times, is desirable in the Church of England." To this an amendment was moved by the Prolocutor as follows: "That the extension of the ministry of women is an urgent need of the Church of England in the present day, and that his Grace the President be prayed to direct the appointment of a Committee to consider the best means by which the systems at present existing may be encouraged, developed, and retained under due control." To this a further amendment was proposed, in the following terms, by the Dean of Manchester, and carried: "That the extension of the ministry of women is an urgent need of the Church of England in the present day, and that the President be prayed to direct the appointment of a Committee to consider the best means by which the work of women may be organised, encouraged, developed, and retained under due control." The speakers, during this debate, were, in order, The Dean of Chester, The Archdeacon of Macclesfield, Canon Body, The Bishop of Durham, Canon Trevor, Canon Tristram, The Prolocutor, The Bishop of Carlisle, The Rev. E. Harman, The Archdeacon of Manchester, Canon Clarke, The President, The Archdeacon of Northumberland, the Archdeacon of Chester, The Archdeacon of Durham, and The Dean of Manchester.

The following Committee was appointed, viz.: The Prolocutor, The Dean of Chester, The Dean of Manchester, The Dean of Ripon, Archdeacon of Auckland, The Archdeacon of Chester, The Archdeacon of Durham, The Archdeacon of the East Riding, The Archdeacon of Macclesfield, The Archdeacon of Manchester, The Archdeacon of Northumberland, Canon Birley, Canon Body, Canon Clarke, Canon Dodd, Canon the Hon. F. R. Grey, Canon Trevór, Canon Ware, and the Rev. E. Harman.

Meetings of this Committee were held on October 1st, 1884, at Carlisle; on October 23d, 1884, at Manchester; and at Leeds, December 8th, 1884, January 7th, 1885, and April 13th, 1885, and the report was presented on the 22d of April.

In moving the adoption of these principles,

THE DEAN OF CHESTER began by saying that no more important subject had ever occupied the attention of this House. Other questions, which had filled the world with their noise—questions of doctrine, questions of ceremonial—had been evanescent. But this question permeated every part of the land and affected every period. They could not touch it without reverting to the earliest Christian times; and what they decided regarding it in that Convocation might hereafter be of the most serious consequence to the Church of England.

Yet the subject had never been discussed in this Synod till last year. He had long been impatient for a debate regarding it and a practical Committee. Now, at last, the opportunity was come. An excellent debate had been secured and a most diligent Committee. Respecting this Committee he must make another remark—and he was sure that Canon Body, who was to second the resolution, would confirm what he said—that throughout their discussions the most brotherly spirit had prevailed. They had been required to deal with topics of the most delicate nature, and not a single unkind word had been spoken by any of them; so that now they could come with their report to the Synod, if he might use such words, "in the fulness of the blessing of the Gospel of Christ."

All that he himself had originally proposed was a resolution having reference to the Primitive Order of Deaconesses, in the hope that a Committee might be appointed to consider the question. But the Prolocutor, with a loftier ambition and a larger scope, proposed to add an inquiry into other kinds of feminine ministration; and the Dean of Manchester, ranging higher and more widely still, proposed and carried the resolution under which the Committee had done their work.

Thus he (the speaker) had prayed for rain and had received the Ganges. He honestly believed that the change in the form of the resolution was a great improvement. Yet it caused no inconsiderable difficulty to the Committee. The resolution was, in fact, in its terms altogether unbounded. To have considered fully all that it included would have been like a multitude of voyages among the stars.

It was absolutely essential for them, as the report stated, to limit their inquiry, and to assign different parts of it to different persons. Regarding some portions it would probably suffice simply to refer to them. He should be sorry, however, if this mere reference were supposed to imply that he had not a due sense of their importance. The growth of ministrations in nursing was one of the most cheering facts of their time; and indications that this change was coming had been seen long ago. The late Dr. Whewell, in his "History of the Inductive Sciences," had shown that there were periods of prelude before actual discoveries were made. So it was here. Thus in Liverpool there had been at a very early period an attempt to form a nursing institution, but the time was not yet ripe. Two of the names connected with this endeavour, were those of Mr. R. Bickersteth, then at the head of the medical profession in that town, and the Rev. Hugh McNeile, afterwards Dean of Ripon. With regard to the system of district visiting, he hoped the paper of Archdeacon Blunt would do much to show its value and to promote its improvement. With respect to Bible-women and parochial Mission-women, he himself had the honour of knowing Mrs. Ranyard, the author of the "Missing Link," and he regarded her, as he regarded Mrs. Pennefather, as one of those women who have the gifts of insight and of organisation, and become the beginners of new and beneficent movements. It seemed to him that in the useful paper due to Mr. Harman more stress might justly have been laid upon the office of the "superintending lady" in work of this kind.

He might now confine his remarks to Deaconesses and Sisterhoods; and even here he would only take a few detached points—three in the former case and two in the latter. But, first, in order to show what thought was in his mind respecting the Deaconess system, he would put it before them in a light in which it had not yet been presented to this assembly. He alluded to the Deaconesses of the Continent. The Church to which they belonged in Germany was Presbyterian, as in Scotland, but with a tendency towards something like Episcopacy. This, of course, must be borne in mind. The number of these Deaconesses was now very large indeed. They were diffused everywhere. It was sometimes, supposed that the only mother house was at Kaiserwerth. This, however, was quite a mistake. There were mother houses at Berlin, Dresden, Hanover, and many other places, to say nothing of Switzerland. And as to the variety of work in which these women were employed he would just give some illustrations which had come before him casually in the course of travelling. At Florence he found one of the best schools for young women of the higher class, conducted by Deaconesses from Kaiserswerth. At Alexandria he found a hospital where our sailors and others were nursed by them; and there those women stood at their post when others were terrified and dispersed at and after the bombardment of the forts. At Beyrout are two Deaconess institutions— one for teaching Syrian girls, another for hospital work. If they wished to know of the institution at Smyrna they would find an account of it in one of Mr. Senior's volumes of "Conversations." And to return to Europe, in the smallest town of Eisenach he asked if there was a Deaconess home, and there he presently found one, where these women were among a company of young cripples, with the customary portraits on the wall of Luther and Melancthon, and of the Crown Prince of Prussia and our own Princess: and so the story might be continued from place to place.

One subject concerning which there was difference of opinion was the practice of setting apart Deaconesses by the laying on of hands. He did not think that this ought to cause any difficulty. This ceremony had a large range and variety of meaning. It was used, for instance, in Confirmation as well as in Ordination. He himself regarded the ordaining of a deacon as very different from the ordaining of a priest; and this was one reason why in a previous debate in this Convocation he had ventured to call in question the modern custom among some of our Bishops of being seated while ordaining priests, which was both a violation of the rubric and also of the universal custom of the Church in East and West. To pursue that subject further would be irrelevant. But it was desirable to put together in their thoughts the appointing of Deacons and the appointing of Deaconesses. It should also be remembered that in the Oriental Church there were services for the latter quite as definite as our service for the former.

The intricate subject of Vows had come out of their deliberations in committee with greater simplicity than might have been expected. They would observe in the report that Canon Body, who understood this subject well, stated that vows were not of the essence even of a Sisterhood. Clearly that word in itself involved no such condition. For his own part he had always contemplated Deaconess work as meant to be a life-work; and he believed it would seldom be abandoned if a long probation were made imperative. Vows of celibacy at an early age involved the utmost peril, with the risk of great scandal; and this was well known to our Bishops, to whose earnest attention this part of the subject was most earnestly and respectfully commended.

Another point, concerning which opinions were not identical, was the value, relatively, of training in Deaconess institutions. He himself was persuaded that if we were to have a thoroughly organised female Diaconate for the Church of England we must have such institutions. The official work of a Deaconess includes a great deal. Besides the acquiring of a knowledge of nursing, and similar qualifications, a Deaconess must acquire some knowledge of herself, and must study the science of co-operation—for it was a science. Yet he thought that there might be a training in the school of experience, of sorrow, and of work, far better than anything that could be learnt in any institution. Let them call to mind the description given by St. Paul of the official "widow," and they would see what he meant. As to controlling our Bishops regarding the women they should appoint as Deaconesses, this was clearly impossible. Moreover it must be recollected that we were now only at the beginning of our enterprise. What might be true with a matured system could hardly be true when we were seeking women of high Christian wisdom to be placed at the head of institutions. We were only as yet digging our wells; and it was premature to insist that all should drink at our thirsty sources.

To turn to Sisterhoods, he could not help remarking that, if Canon Body was correct—and he did not doubt that he was correct—that in ancient times the consecration of a Sister could only come from a Bishop, then it was to be doubted whether some English Sisterhoods were Sisterhoods at all in any true ecclesiastical sense—whether they were not voluntary societies outside the regular life of the Church. So with regard to the real control exercised by Bishops over Sisterhoods. He himself remembered very well his perplexity on visiting Clewer many years ago after hearing what Bishop Wilberforce said at the Oxford Church Congress. His other remark on this subject had reference to the distrust and suspicion frequently caused by what appeared to be mere imitations of the modern Church at Rome. A defined dress for women appointed to an office of this kind he regarded as quite imperative. But it could not be wise to hinder so good a cause by adopting costumes which probably did as much harm to women in one way as the extreme of fashion did in another. So with respect to the use of words. He would only take two examples—the employment of the terms "religion" and "chastity." As to the former, he thought that venerable theologian and accomplished scholar, Archbishop Trench, had given them some very wise instruction. As to the latter, surely it might foster a subtle and morbid Pharisaism if a young woman were taught that because she was under a vow of celibacy therefore she was more chaste than the mother who bore her. What he hoped for was that their committee might last to the end of this Convocation, with the addition of some of the Bishops, on whom must rest the chief responsibility of the subject, and who would have the most serious experience of its difficulties.

The speakers in order were the Dean of Chester, Canon Ware, Canon Trevor, Canon Clarke, Canon

Body, Canon Knowles, The Archbishop of Macclesfield, The Archdeacon of Auckland, Canon Tristram, The Dean of Durham, The Archdeacon of the East Riding, The Archdeacon of Chester, and the Dean of Manchester.

The proposed resolutions were agreed to.

On this occasion the two Houses sat separately. The Archdeacon of the East Riding moved the following resolution, which was seconded by Canon Body, and carried:—" That the President be humbly requested to add to this Committee, such Members of the Upper House as he sees fit, so that a joint Committee of the whole Synod may be ready to take advantage of any discussion upon this or kindred subjects in the Convocation of Canterbury."

THE DEAN OF CHESTER, in replying, said he hoped the House would take note of a remark which fell from Canon Body, that the Bishop of Durham had convinced him that Deaconesses were a regularly constituted part of the ministry of the Apostolic Church, and that such a conviction coloured a man's whole view of the subject. This, the speaker said, had been his own state of mind during more than twenty years.

As to the imposition of hands he merely wished to add this, that the Deaconesses of the Continent were set apart in this way, as had been all Deaconesses hitherto in the Church of England. He thought there was much force in the Dean of Manchester's observation, that there must be some outward visible gesture on such an occasion, and that no gesture was so suitable as this.

Canon Trevor had quoted an early description of part of the work of Primitive Deaconesses, to show that those early times differed from our own. But this did not prove that Deaconesses did not do other kinds of work. If a Clergyman was described as a preacher, it did not follow that he did not visit the sick. If Canon Trevor would search his own stores of learning, and they were copious, he would remember how Chrysostom's life in Constantinople, and on his journeys, showed that he had around him a large number of these ministers, who did very varied work.

Canon Tristram's fear lest strict Episcopal supervision should bring in dangerous customs did not move him. There was not much fear of inquisitorial tyranny on the part of the Bishops. There was far more reason to dread that they would not look closely enough into this subject. As to "inner rules," his friend had mistaken the meaning of the term. It had no reference to cookery, but to the direction of the spiritual life. To look at this subject aright we must turn from the kitchen to the chapel.

Much had been said about removing certain words regarding vows from one of the recommendations; but it had been rightly argued that the retention of them showed that the recommending of vows of celibacy was not in the Report at all.

The reference to the "moving by the Holy Ghost" —a subject to be touched with the utmost reverence —had been objected to; but something of this kind was requisite in order to lift up this whole subject into that highest sphere within which alone it was safe to contemplate it.

The Dean concluded by expressing his extreme gratitude to the friends who, in the course of the debate, had spoken of him so kindly.

WORKS on HOME and FOREIGN MISSIONS, EVANGELISTIC WORK, &c. &c.

IN THE SLUMS. Pages from the Note-Book of a London Diocesan Home Missionary. By the Rev. D. RICE-JONES, M.A. Small crown 8vo, 2s. 6d.

ADDRESSES TO DISTRICT VISITORS AND SUNDAY-SCHOOL TEACHERS. By FRANCIS PIGOU, D.D., Vicar of Halifax. With a Preface by the Right Rev. the Bishop of ROCHESTER. Small crown 8vo, 2s.

SEEKING THE LOST: Incidents and Sketches of Christian Work in London. By the Rev. C. J. WHITMORE. Crown 8vo, 3s. 6d.

SEEKING AFTER GOD. By the Rev. C. J. WHITMORE. 16mo, 1s.

HASTE TO THE RESCUE; or, Work While it is Day. By Mrs. CHARLES WIGHTMAN. Crown 8vo, 1s. 6d.

BY THE SAME AUTHOR.

ANNALS OF THE RESCUED. With a Preface by the Rev. C. E. L. WIGHTMAN. Crown 8vo, 3s. 6d.

ARREST THE DESTROYER'S MARCH. Crown 8vo, 3s. 6d.

WORKERS AT HOME. By Mrs. WIGLEY, Author of "Our Home Work." Crown 8vo, 5s.

Separately, as follows, 1s. each.

THOUGHTS FOR MOTHERS.
THOUGHTS FOR CHILDREN.
THOUGHTS FOR SERVANTS.
THOUGHTS FOR TEACHERS.
THOUGHTS FOR YOUNG WOMEN IN BUSINESS.

RAGGED HOMES, AND HOW TO MEND THEM. By Mrs. BAYLY, Author of "The Story of our English Bible," &c. Crown 8vo, 1s. 6d.

"We scarcely know which to praise most highly, the matter or the manner of this work. The author's style is as attractive as her subject. Mrs. Bayly has wrought with an artist's eye and spirit."—*Daily News.*

THE HAPPY HOME. By JAMES HAMILTON, D.D. New Edition. With Illustrations. 18mo, 1s. 6d.

CONTENTS:—The Friend of the People—The Ship of Neaver—A Bunch in the Hand and More in the Bush—The Oasis—The Fireside—Day Dreaming—Fire Flies—The Faithful Tenant—The True Disciple.

THE MISSING LINK; or, Bible Women in the Homes of the London Poor. By L. N. R., Author of "The Book and its Story." Crown 8vo, 3s. 6d. A Cheaper Edition, 1s. 6d.

BY THE SAME AUTHOR.

NURSES FOR THE NEEDY; or, The Bible Women Nurses in the Homes of the London Poor. Crown 8vo, 3s. 6d.

COMFORT : A Book for the Cottage. By JANE BESEMERES. 16mo, 1s.

OUR COFFEE-ROOM. By Lady HOPE. With Preface by Lieutenant-General Sir ARTHUR COTTON, R.E., K.C.S.I. Crown 8vo, 3s. 6d.

BY THE SAME AUTHOR.

MORE ABOUT "OUR COFFEE-ROOM." Crown 8vo, 3s. 6d.

The late Earl CAIRNS said—"It was one of the most interesting stories he had ever had the pleasure of reading, and showed what a lady could do when she undertook and rightly worked a design and place of that kind with such objects."

LINES OF LIGHT ON A DARK BACKGROUND. Crown 8vo, 3s. 6d.

"Calculated to be of signal service to all who are labouring in the temperance cause."—*Churchman's Magazine.*

LIFE IN HOSPITAL. By a SISTER. 16mo, 1s.

"This little book should be read by all. It is far too brief; that is its one fault."—*London Quarterly Review.*

HINTS TO HOSPITAL AND SICK-ROOM VISITORS. By Mrs. COLIN G. CAMPBELL. Crown 8vo, 1s. 6d.

BRIGHT GLIMPSES FOR MOTHERS' MEETINGS. By a MOTHER. With a Preface by the Rev. THOMAS VORES, late Vicar of St. Mary's, Hastings. Crown 8vo, 1s. 6d.

BY THE SAME AUTHOR.

PRAYERS FOR MOTHERS' MEETINGS. 16mo, 6d.; paper cover, 3d.

HOME THOUGHTS FOR MOTHERS AND MOTHERS' MEETINGS. By the Author of "Sick-bed Vows, and How to Keep Them." Crown 8vo, 1s. 6d.

NELLIE: A Story of Prison Life. By Mrs. MEREDITH. Crown 8vo, 1s. 6d.

BY THE SAME AUTHOR.

A BOOK ABOUT CRIMINALS. Crown 8vo, 3s. 6d.

FURTHER RECOLLECTIONS OF AN INDIAN MISSIONARY. By the Rev. C. B. LEUPOLT. With Portrait and other Illustrations. Crown 8vo, 5s.

"Mr. Leupolt's 'Recollections' are recorded in a truthful and manly form, and are well worthy of perusal, all the more so as they are mostly cast in a rather systematic form under different heads, including a short but deeply interesting chapter on the Indian Mutiny."—*Church Bells.*

THIRTY-EIGHT YEARS' MISSION LIFE IN JAMAICA: A Brief Sketch of the Rev. WARRAND CARLILE, Missionary at Brownsville. By one of his SONS. Small crown 8vo, 3s. 6d.

SOUTH AFRICA AND ITS MISSION FIELDS. By the Rev. J. E. CARLYLE, late Presbyterian Minister and Chaplain, Natal. Post 8vo, 5s.

THE WHITE FIELDS OF FRANCE: An Account of Mr. M'All's Mission to the Working Men of Paris. By HORATIUS BONAR, D.D. Crown 8vo, 3s. 6d.

BY THE SAME AUTHOR.

DOES GOD CARE FOR OUR GREAT CITIES? A Word for the Paris Mission. 18mo, 9d.

THE RESPONSIBILITY OF THE HEATHEN AND THE RESPONSIBILITY OF THE CHURCH. By the Rev. C. F. CHILDE, M.A., Rector of Holbrook, Suffolk. 16mo, 1s.

VEDIC RELIGION. By the Rev. K. S. MACDONALD, Missionary of the Free Church of Scotland, Calcutta. Small crown 8vo, 3s. 6d.

HINDU WOMEN, with Glimpses into their Life and Zenanas. By Miss H. LLOYD, Editorial Secretary of the Church of England Zenana Missionary Society. Crown 8vo, 2s. 6d.

ROMANCE OF MISSIONS IN BITHYNIA. By MARIA A. WEST. Crown 8vo, 1s. 6d.

"One of the most interesting of missionary books—the very thing for reading at working parties, or for the Sunday-school library."—*Sword and Trowel.*

MISSIONS TO THE WOMEN OF CHINA, in Connection with the Society for Promoting Female Education in the East. Crown 8vo, cloth, 2s.

GOD'S ANSWERS: The Narrative of Miss Annie Macpherson's Work at the Home of Industry, Spitalfields. By Miss LOWE. With Illustrations. Crown 8vo, 3s. 6d.

REMARKABLE ANSWERS TO PRAYER. By JOHN RICHARDSON PHILLIPS, formerly Country Association Agent for the London City Mission. Crown 8vo, 3s. 6d.

BY THE SAME AUTHOR.

REMARKABLE PROVIDENCES AND PROOFS OF A DIVINE REVELATION. With Thoughts, Facts, and Anecdotes Calculated to Strengthen Faith. Fifth Edition. With Illustrations. Crown 8vo, 3s. 6d.

REMARKABLE CASES OF CONVERSION AND OTHER EXPERIENCES, showing the Value of Faith in the Faithful Promiser. Crown 8vo, 3s. 6d.

PLEASANT FRUITS; or, Records of the Cottage and the Class. By MARIA V. G. HAVERGAL. Seventh Edition. Crown 8vo, 2s. 6d.

TERSE TALKS ON TIMELY TOPICS. By HENRY VARLEY. Crown 8vo, 3s. 6d.

ILLUSTRATIVE SCRIPTURE READINGS: A Manual for Visitation and Devotion. By the Rev. T. E. COZENS COOKE. 16mo, 2s.; roan, 3s.

GEMS FROM THE BIBLE: Being Selections Convenient for Reading to the Sick and Aged. Crown 8vo, 3s. 6d.

COTTAGE READINGS IN THE BOOK OF EXODUS. Crown 8vo, 5s.

THE CHRISTIAN VISITOR'S TEXT-BOOK. By the Rev. CHARLES NEIL, M.A. Crown 8vo, 2s.

THE VISITOR'S BOOK OF TEXTS; or, The Word brought Nigh to the Sick and Sorrowful. By A. A. BONAR, D.D. Sixth Edition. Crown 8vo, 3s. 6d.

INVITATIONS. By Lady HOPE. 16mo, 1s. 6d. In a packet, 16mo, 1s.; separately, 2d. each.

AWAKENING AND INVITING CALLS. Tracts. By the Very Rev. HENRY LAW, M.A., late Dean of Gloucester. 16mo, 6d.

THE SINNER'S FRIEND. By J. V. HALL. 32mo, 1d., 2d., and 3d. Large type, 6d. paper cover; 1s. cloth limp; 1s. 6d. cloth gilt.

OF WHAT DOES IT CONSIST? or, The Elements of Saving Truth in "A Basket of Fragments and Crumbs." By Lieutenant-Colonel M. J. ROWLANDSON. 16mo, 1s. 6d.

ENGLISH HEARTS AND ENGLISH HANDS; or, The Railway and the Trenches. By Miss MARSH. Crown 8vo, 5s. Cheaper Edition, 2s.

<small>The *Times*, referring to Miss Marsh's books, has said—" The Memorials of Vicars and these memorials of the Crystal Palace navvies are books of precisely the same type. We recognise in them an honesty of purpose, a purity of heart, and a warmth of human affection, combined with a religious faith that are very beautiful."</small>

BY THE SAME AUTHOR.

WHAT MIGHT HAVE BEEN: A True Story. 1s.

FROM DARK TO DAWN; or, The Story of Warwick Roland. 2d. sewed; 4d. limp cloth; 6d. gilt edges.

DREAMLIGHT FROM HEAVEN AND HEAVENLY REALITIES. 16mo, 6d.

MIDNIGHT CHIMES; or, The Voice of Hope. 1d.

DEATH AND LIFE: Records of the Cholera Wards in the London Hospital. 6d.; paper cover, 3d.

BRAVE, KIND, AND HAPPY: Words of Hearty Friendship to the Working Men of England. 1d.

LIGHT FOR THE LINE; or, The Story of Thomas Ward, a Railway Workman. 6d.; paper cover, 4d.

THE GOLDEN CHAIN. 1s. 6d.; paper cover, 6d.

THE RIFT IN THE CLOUDS. 1s.

CROSSING THE RIVER. 1s.

SHINING LIGHT. 1s.

THE RACE AND THE PRIZE. 1d.

READY. 1d.

HEROES OF THE MINE. 9d.

THE DAY DAWN. 1d.

THE HAVEN AND THE HOME. 6d.; paper cover, 3d.

WORDS OF HEARTY FRIENDSHIP TO SOLDIERS, SAILORS, AND WORKING MEN, containing—Death and Life; Light for the Line; The Haven and the Home; Brave, Kind, and Happy; The Race and the Prize; Ready; Day Dawn; Midnight Chimes. In Packets, price 1s.

LONDON: JAMES NISBET & CO., 21 BERNERS STREET.

This book is a preservation photocopy.
It is made in compliance with copyright law
and produced on acid-free archival
60# book weight paper
which meets the requirements of
ANSI/NISO Z39.48-1992 (permanence of paper)

Preservation photocopying and binding
by
Acme Bookbinding
Charlestown, Massachusetts
📖
2000

CPSIA information can be obtained
at www.ICGtesting.com
Printed in the USA
LVOW13s0529010818
585579LV00007B/95/P

9 781376 289770